Trying Times

Based on true story

Tilahun Tassew

Publishing History

Trying Times was originally published in 2011 by Shama Books, a division of Shama PLC with ISBN: 978-99944-0-058-4
Second Edition Create Space Amazon Books paperback published in February 2013

All right reserved.
Copy right © Tilahun Tassew, 2011

Hard cover edition ISBN: 9798791318015

Kindle Direct Publishing of hard cover 2021

Many people have extended indispensable support during the preparation of this book. Thanks go to the editor Sian Jackson-Harman, and to Tesfaye Haile Michael, Mesfin Temesgen, Gebeyehu Tassew, Desta Wolde Kidan, Getachew Wondim Agengehu, Fenoteyeman Birhan, Merawi Goshu, Wosen Seged Negussie, Dr Abiy Tsegaye and Oumoukan Bagayoko.

In cherished memory of
Defabachew Tassew (1939-1978)

Not certain, it will outlast a day,
  one season, years or ages.
I am building this monument,
  from collapsed gravestones, strewn everywhere;
    piece to piece cemented by blood and tears.

It will honor fallen heroes and non-combatants,
  who were confident and hoped,
To be sung by millions, for the cause for which they died,
  and the love they bestowed.

I will erect it here in this high place,
    and leisurely walk away,
knowing for sure somebody will stand by;
    and compose himself humbly;
      to glorify the fight for love, loyalty,
        freedom and dignity.

"The man who took the lid off" a cartoon by David Low about Mussolini's incursion into Ethiopia, alluding to the Pandora's Box in Greek Mythology, 4 October 1935.

Part One: War and Little Ladies 9
Part Two: War and Soldiers 60
Part 3: Heroes Come to Villages 83
Part Four: War, Life and Love 94
Part Five: Patriotism and War 121
Part Six: The Comrade in Arms 148
Part Seven: War and Love 175
Part Eight: War and Destiny 190
Part Nine: War, Love and Responsibility 218
Part Ten: The Tides Change 227

In 1935, the Italian fascist government invaded Ethiopia and started chemical warfare. One of the chemical war martyrs was a soldier from a tiny isolated village in central Ethiopia. Shortly afterward, contingents of the Ethiopian army arrived in the remote village of the Martyr and began a partisan war against the occupation army of fascist Italy. Two little girls joined the partisan fighters to avenge their uncle soldier who was killed in a chemical attack on a remote battlefield. Thus, not only the life and fate of the two little girls, but also the little villagers and warrior partisans were completely transformed. Based on the girls' true story, this is said and recalled for generations.

Part One: War and Little Ladies
Meseret and Mahlet

1

Meseret, a sixteen-year-old girl, stood at the edge of the vast prairie where the magnificent Adabai River gorge that runs in a southwesterly direction to join the Blue Nile River begins. She contemplated the open prairie that stretched away to the horizon. She remembered standing with her uncle Samson in the same spot a year earlier. He had put his left hand around her and his daughter Mahlet while pointing with his right hand towards the town of Sasit.

"From here, about 600 kilometers north in the same direction lies Tigrai, where I am going to fight the Fascist Italians," she remembered her uncle announcing to them. He pointed to the North-Eastern direction beyond the horizon to Yifat, where the two girls had visited a week earlier with Meseret's mother. "If you would stand on the cliffs in Yifat you could see Hararghe and beyond that Ogaden. My friend has already left for the Ogaden to fight the Italians."

He then pointed to the south, his arms still resting on their shoulders, to the Adabai gorge. She remembered him pointing out to them a hill further from the gorge towards the town of Molale. "If you could fly and connect Molale with Sasit and Robe in Yifat in straight lines you would have a triangle." She remembered him drawing a triangle on the field with the spear he held. "Look, that is a triangle," he had said.

Her eyes filled in tears she remembered when he took each of them by their two hands and swung them around with him, telling them they were drawing circles. He joked about Meseret being skinny and Mahlet plump. He had completed the education given by the church and earlier had attended the first modern school opened in Addis Ababa.

Meseret's uncle, along with most of his family members, had left after few days to the warfront, to fight the Italians in the north. That was almost a year ago.

Meseret felt lonely and sad. She recalled the memory of her uncle and the other relatives who had gone to the war in the north a year earlier. The memory appeared to her like a mirage, and then slowly drifted away.

She recalled the day when relatives of the warriors had bid them farewell, watching them until they disappeared into the horizon. She remembered how she brought his horse, first riding it awhile before handing it over to him. She remembered his gentleness when he took the horse and how agile he was when mounting it. She remembered her uncle leading the way on his horse with another brother following him on foot. She imagined them shooting and killing their enemies. She let her imagination drift as she anticipated being ambushed and their blood being spilled.

Two years earlier, she had seen the blood of her uncle on a stone, drying after a gunfight. It awoke a horrendous feeling of rage and revenge within her heart. She wondered why that spilled blood, of all the blood she had seen, created such appalling wrath within her. She had discussed the emotion with her uncle Samson and he explained about the strength of blood ties. She remembered their conversation and felt the same anger and desire for revenge she had felt upon seeing his blood. She clasped her hands and put them on her breasts as she always did when she was agitated or sad.

Trying to cleanse her soul from the overwhelming feelings of hatred that had engulfed her, she raised her eyes to the sky and prayed to God's blessing and the safe return of her uncle and his followers.

Meseret walked sadly near the edge of the escarpment and turned her face to the gorge. It was a marvelous site created by the Adabai River and its tributaries extended down hundreds of meters. From where she stood, the other side of the gorge rose to a mountainous height. On the steps of the gorge, villages were scattered on every level. Midway up the side of the gorge, facing her was Geregera village where she was born. Her father, Kahn Wondimu, and most of the relatives on his side of the family were priests and all lived in Geregera.

Mahlet, the fifteen-year-old daughter of Uncle Samson, born out of wedlock, climbed the escarpment and stood quietly beside Meseret. She turned her eyes to follow Meseret's gaze and fell into the same pensive mood.

The somber feeling in the air was palpable, and Mahlet, desperately wanting to raise the spirit of her friend, sang a song that their grandfather had written.

"From the bean fields,
Let us go to the virgin lands;
From this endless plain,
Let us climb uninhabited mountains.
Or like a bandit with a rifle,
Run together to Adabai River in the gorges.

[12]
Or like a crow, a swan, fly in the air over the prairie."

"Our grandmother is approaching," Meseret said in an attempt to scare Mahlet and stop her from singing. Meseret's grandmother did not like the song repeated, especially by Mahlet.

"Oh God!" said Mahlet in fear, relaxing after seeing no one approaching. She appreciated the teasing and started to run down the cliff, challenging Meseret to a race to reach the church compound first. Meseret unclasped her hands and ran down the zigzagging trail with buoyant energy. They were laughing and chanting jubilantly in stark contrast to the somber emotions that filled their hearts a few moments ago.

When the two girls reached the church, they saw that all the villagers had gathered for Sunday morning worship at the small, circular, thatched-roof building. Some of the villagers were praying with their faces touching the outer walls of the church, while most were praying with their faces resting on the outer circular fence of the church. They were all, however, facing the holy of holies where the tabot, the symbol for the Ark of the Covenant, rested. The people stood humbly in reverence, certain that their God would neither forsake them nor confer upon them unbearable calamities. According to their beliefs, only those who had committed transgressions in open defiance of God's commandments would suffer the consequences. Since the fascist invasion of Ethiopia, they had asked their God to watch over them with mercy, grant protection and victory to their beloved warriors. They were also praying for valor to the Emperor's armies fighting throughout the countryside.

Meseret and Mahlet joined the family and stood in the row behind their grandmother, Taitu. Meseret had long observed that her family circle had become very small after her uncle went to the war with his kins and followers. Other families were attending the service, but the numbers of her family in attendance were fewer. She tried to stop her thoughts from wandering to these painful feelings and concentrate on the Sunday sermon.

A new priest, named Kahn Yohannes, was giving the Sunday sermon. He was one of the few educated elites of the church. They used the term Kahn to refer to priest Yohannes, as is a title signifying priests who dedicate themselves to the service of the Ark of the Covenant. He had returned from the northern front with the remnants of the Emperor's army, praying and making supplication to God in all the churches, especially in the rock-hewn churches of Lalibela, which he passed before settling in Nib Washa to serve in the nearby Saint Mary church in Jer.

Kahn Yohannes used the occasion to attack the fascist's racist ideology. He based his sermon on the Glory of Kings, the Book that describes the story of how the Ark of the Covenant arrived in Ethiopia from Jerusalem during the time of King Solomon. He began his sermon by assuring the multitude that Ethiopia, as the resting place of the Ark of the Covenant, is a blessed country protected by God's promises and that soon the Almighty would have his revenge on the Italian invaders.

He reviled the Italian fascists for considering themselves as superior human beings destined to civilize the chosen people of God, the Ethiopians. "The Italian Fascists consider themselves as superior human beings destined to civilize the chosen people of God. Before God, all men are equal. God prefers those who are of the highest moral standard. The fascists are lowly characters. We have witnessed their barbarity during the battles in the north and southeast Ethiopia". He concluded his sermon.

The priest looked at his congregation, and then suddenly, the specter of the Battle of Maichew, where the Italians in their victory were wreaking death and destruction upon Ethiopians, flashed through his mind. He shuddered, but in reverence for the mercy of God, he told his congregation that God had not forsaken his people and that God's promise is everlasting.

Soon afterward, the sermon ended with the Lord's Prayer. "Our father who art in heaven, hallowed be thy name; thy kingdom come, thy will be done on earth..."

When the mass ended, the people began to leave for their homes. Many families walked Taitu to the junction leading to her home. Meseret felt gratitude to the people of her village and the neighboring areas.

Meseret and Mahlet remained behind and began to chat. They sat on the meadow and talked about the rumors they had overheard from the elders.

"I overheard the soldiers who returned from the war talking about airplanes and how people burned to ashes when exposed to the rain from the airplane", Mahlet told Meseret in a low voice.

"Liquid does not burn something, it is only fire that burns and it turns to ash whatever it touches it." Meseret tried to correct her.

"The Italian's liquid must be different or maybe they were talking about fire." Mahlet answered, and confirmed that she had also heard that people were being burnt to ashes in the war fields. However, the topic sent a chill of terror through both of them.

Mahlet did not like to harbor such feelings for long. She challenged Meseret to reach the house first. They ran down the escarpment to the house, competing in earnest.

Meseret abruptly opened the door of her house, mocking Mahlet for losing the race. As Meseret burst in, she unceremoniously disturbed the quiet setting of a get-together taking place in the living room, where two guests were drinking coffee with her grandmother.

"Sorry," said Meseret, blushing in embarrassment.

"Do you remember him?" her grandmother asked, pointing to the elderly guest. "He is a relative who left for the frontier lands with your uncle, my son, Samson, ten years ago, when you were still a child. He has finally returned to his birthplace. Go and greet him."

Meseret's grandmother, Taitu began to cry, remembering that her son who left for Maichew never returned. "Nobody can tell me whether he is dead or alive. All say that they never saw him dead," said Taitu sobbing.

"Is there anybody in your village who has returned from Maichew?" Taitu asked the other guest as she always did whenever she encountered a stranger.

"Not lately," said the old man. Everybody except Taitu believed her son had died a year earlier. The old man did not want to tell her, but he had witnessed the martyrdom of her son

[16]
seven months ago during the Ethiopian Christmas counteroffensive prior to the Battle of Maichew.

Her son and his 50 followers were amongst the three victorious Ethiopian battalions during the first days of the Christmas counteroffensive. They were planning to crush the Italians once and for all. Suddenly airplanes appeared in the faraway sky. Samson expected them to throw barrels filled with mustard gas instead they sprayed them with a colorless liquid that causes suffocation. The airplanes started spraying the whole battleground with a brownish gelatinous substance and then they bombed the whole area with flamethrowers[1]. There were no ground troops to fight with and the airplanes were unreachable by gunfire. A hundred thousand Ethiopian soldiers were suffocated or burned[2].

---

[1] The nature of the "special liquid", as wrote by Marshal Graziani of Fascist Italy, came to light after this book was published. Graziani explained the importance of what he called the special liquid in a recent document acquired by the Library of Congress (Bridget Conley August 29, 2012): Marshall Graziani wrote that the special liquid was "Essential condition for the succeeding of the Operation: (....) the free use of special-liquid bombs and shells in order to inflict maximum losses on the enemy, and above all to effect his complete collapse of morale"

[2] One of the commanders of the Ethiopian army Leul Ras Kassa shed light on the nature of the "special liquid" in his interview with Marcel Griaule in 1936 as follows:
"Thick fog falls like rain sprayed over us and the surrounding area was engulfed in fire. The brownish liquid ate the flesh of the soldiers. It was difficult even to mention the number of people who perished. The Ethiopian heroic soldiers died without leaving their

[17]

The martyrs died in great anguish. The old man avoided telling Taitu about the death of her son and his soldiers, not wanting to cause her pain or disclose the details of the circumstances of Samson and his soldiers' tragic demise.

"How was Addis Ababa after the Emperor left? Are all our relatives in Addis Ababa safe?" Taitu asked. The old man was glad that the conversation had changed from her son to a more general topic.

"God is merciful; most are alive and well," he said. "Addis Ababa has turned to a death field."

"We heard first the news about the battle fought to retake Addis Ababa from the Italians and then the bombs thrown at the Italian viceroy in Addis Ababa and then the massacre by the Italians."

"Yes, that was true. Two months after Emperor Haile Selassie left to Europe the Ethiopian armies that were stationed in the surrounding rural areas tried to recapture Addis Ababa. The offensive failed, but it gave a shock to the Italians who had declared that they occupied the whole of Ethiopia."

The elderly visitor and Taitu continued the discussion about the situation in the country. Meseret sat on the carpet near Taitu and followed the discussion.

"I think it is better to encircle the cities and fight the Italians when they try to move out to the rural areas rather than trying to take over the cities and towns," said the visitor. Taitu

---

assigned positions. Mules, cows, sheep and wild animals threw themselves into cliffs and died.(Laketch p 66/68)

was not happy about what he said. She considered the ousting of the Italians from the cities and towns equally important.

The other elderly visitor supported the view of his friend. He started to describe what had happened after the Emperor's return to Addis Ababa from the Northern front. He told her about the Imperial decree to move the capital city from Addis Ababa to Gore in the South West. He also told her how it was decreed that all provincial governors were to undertake counteroffensive measures and move their headquarters outside the provincial capitals and into the rural areas. Meanwhile, the Emperor used his political prowess to try to mobilize support in the League of Nations. He concluded that a strategy to recapture Addis Ababa would not be in line with the Imperial decree.

"I heard that General Kebede, the commander of Menz, Tegulet, and Yifat army, is leading the war around here very well. They say we can continue our lives as usual because his warriors had prevented the Italians from penetrating the rural villages. Do you think this will continue?" she asked.

"I hope so," said the elderly man. He also added that he was aware that General Kebede was her relative on her mother's side.

"Yes, it is true. He sends me greetings and good wishes occasionally. I met him when he came from Addis Ababa under the instructions of the Emperor. He launched a big military show in the prairie above our home. He was standing gracefully while the Menz army, led by Gizachew, arrived in a parade. When they came nearer to him, Gizachew held his machinegun in his right hand and saluted him, traditionally bowing to the ground. Gizachew's followers bowed at the same time. He bade them rise and greeted them. It must be a demonstration of allegiance for their commander. Beshah, leading the Tegulet army and Tessema, leading the Yifat army, did the same. It was very impressive."

"It was very nice. The village boys try to mimic the occasion, so do we girls," said Meseret.

Taitu was not particularly interested in Meseret's comment; she continued addressing the old man, "Do you think General Kebede army will be able to keep the Italians away from the rural lands?"

"With God's help," he answered, to remind her that glory is only from God.

"I will pray for him and his soldiers' safety when I pray for the safe return of my son Samson," she concluded.

Mahlet entered the room. "Who is this girl?" asked the old man. "Is she our relative? Whose daughter is she?" insisted the old man who could only understand individuals in their family setting.

"She is the daughter of our Kejele," said Taitu, Meseret's grandmother emphasizing 'our Kejele' to give a belittling meaning.

Meseret's face reddened with anger by this comment, but she did not respond.

"Who is this Kejele? Is this Kejele the same one that your son brought back from the South? She is a very nice lady," said the old man who rose, approached Mahlet, and kissed her on her forehead.

Taitu knew the undying love of her son for Kejele. She had been unsuccessful in marrying him to one of the ladies of the big local families.

Her persistent reference to Kejele as a servant was not a hindrance to him. "Kejele is our servant. She was Meseret's nanny, when Meseret was a child. Meseret's mother Eleni had left her to me when she was a child. Meseret speaks Kejele's language like Amharic. She considers Kejele as her mother and Mahlet as her sister," said Taitu.

The old man saw uneasiness on Meseret's face. He too felt uneasy and tried to change the topic. "By the way Meseret, your uncle Commander Beshah is currently in Sasit, they say he is preparing for an upcoming battle," said the old man.

"Please tell him that I will come and visit him soon," said Meseret.

Her grandmother took it as a good childish prank. The grandmother seemed to hear defiance in her grandchild's tone.

"You are blessed girl, Meseret. I think of you as I do of the brave warriors fighting for our country. Such girls are needed in such times," said the first elderly visitor. He believed that whenever women supported a war in earnest and dared to take arms, victory was inevitable.

That night, Meseret could not sleep. She recalled the new preacher's sermon about the coming of the Ark of the Covenant to Ethiopia. She tried to capture every word the Kahn was saying about the chosen people of God. This brought back another memory of the time she had passed in Yifat with her mother a year earlier.

She had gone to Yifat with Mahlet and her mother under unusual circumstances. A year earlier, before the occupation of Addis Ababa by the Italians, Eleni, Meseret's mother, came from Addis Ababa to their village called Nib Washa.

Nib Washa, just below the escarpment after the vast prairie, got its name, (literally meaning 'Cave of the Honey Bee') from the wild honeybee colonies found in the cave near the village. Meseret's mother, feeling restless after her two days stay in Nib Washa, decided to go to Yifat to visit her property there. The trip too enabled mother and daughter to know each other better.

The mother asked Meseret and Mahlet to accompany her on her visit to Yifat. The two girls agreed out of curiosity; they were intrigued by Eleni's unusual disposition. She greeted everybody and seemed to be interested in every detail around her.

One Sunday she took them to the church in Yifat. As she lay in her bed half-asleep, Meseret remembered the preacher in the Yifat church. He had been narrating about Debre Orit, the resting place of the Ark of the Covenant. He said that Ethiopia, like Debre Orit was a blessed country. He even said that Ethiopia had been a blessed country before Christianity. Meseret lay awake remembering how the speech had affected her.

When they were returning from the Church Meseret's mother, Eleni had greeted the Sheik of the Grand Mosque in Yifat who was coming towards them. She had chatted with the Sheik in her jovial mood. Meseret had interrupted their discussion and asked the Sheik "Was Ethiopia a blessed land before Islam?" Meseret's mother was shocked. She did not know why the girl asked the question. She reprimanded her. However, the Sheik said "It is okay. She is an intelligent girl. Our prophet sent his followers to Ethiopia identifying it as a land of justice and bliss." Meseret smiled to herself as she lay in her bed. Her thoughts drifted to her uncle Beshah who was commanding the army battalion in Sasit not far from Nib Washa. Eventually, she fell asleep. She awoke after a while feeling distressed; she woke Mahlet to share her idea with her. Meseret asked Mahlet if she would accompany her on a journey to visit their uncle, Commander Beshah, and join the Ethiopian army fighting the Italians.

Mahlet laughed. She thought the idea childish. "Please leave me alone. I want to sleep a little bit," she said turning her back on Meseret.

Meseret felt bad. She felt rejected by her closest friend. She did not want to discuss the issue with Mahlet anymore. She decided to leave on her own for Commander Beshah's military camp in Sasit in the morning.

She felt not only lonely but also afraid in the wide and quiet prairie. Her footsteps were audible to her. However, she controlled her fear and continued marching.

To Meseret's delight, it was not long before her feelings of loneliness vanished, for Mahlet caught up with her, running from behind and trying to catch he breath. Meseret was ecstatic. She embraced Mahlet and kissed her as if they were meeting after a long separation. When Mahlet had recovered herself, they ran together across the wide expanse that stretched from Nib Washa to Sasit, where Commander Beshah had established his command post. The girls laughed with sheer ebullience.

When their grandmother Taitu heard about their departure from home, without her knowledge, she was very angry. Nevertheless, as time passed she started considering Meseret and Mahlet as heroines that would avenge her gallant son, Samson, who never returned from the northern front along with his soldiers.

2

It had taken Meseret and Mahlet five hours to reach Sasit. The people in Sasit were all out in the field and everybody was busy. The two girls came to an abrupt stop as they viewed the scene before them. Commander Beshah sat astride a white horse while moving around giving orders. Meseret was able to understand some of the Commander's speech, from where they stood, even though he suffered from a stutter, but to Mahlet it was a mystery. Commander Beshah was sending his men on a mission. "Hurry up and tell Commander Gizachew Haile and Commander Tessema that we are leaving for Tamra-Ber. Hurry up," he commanded. Completely focused on the battle preparation, Commander Beshah did not recognize Meseret and Mahlet. He seemed to see all and no one in particular.

Meseret watched her uncle with admiration. He was legendary as the commander who had inflicted heavy damage on the Italian Army as it hastened to occupy Addis Ababa a year earlier. Commander Beshah, as a farewell to his enemies, attacked the rear guard, destroyed many transport vehicles, killed a lot of Italians, and retreated from the highways before finally establishing his command post here in Sasit.

"You are Commander Beshah's sister, or am I mistaken?" asked an old woman. The woman referred to Meseret as a sister of Beshah because all relatives in Ethiopia are traditionally referred sisters and brothers. "Your brother is a brave man," she added

"Commander Tessema is also coming. He is also your brother, isn't he?"

"Yes, he is."

"Kefelew will also come."

She smiled. She thought to herself that he would be happy to see her and Mahlet. When he came to visit their grandmother, he usually chatted with them.

Meseret and Mahlet felt at home, perhaps because they knew many of the legendary warriors that were fighting the enemy. Most of their family members were army commanders. They also felt as if they had become members of an Ethiopian army contingent.

The supreme commander of all in Yifat, Tegulet, and Menz was General Kebede, also a relative of theirs. The girls had never met him but he often sent messages and letters to their grandmother, Taitu.

General Kebede, the supreme commander of the Yifat, Tegulet, and Menz army, was one of the elderly people of the palace. He had established his command center in Molale. He stationed his battalions under the command of Gizachew in Menz, Beshah in Tegulet, and Tesema in Yifat in a triangular formation, frustrating the Italian attempt to penetrate the countryside on the left and right side of the Asmara-Addis Ababa main route. If the Italians tried to penetrate Yifat by attacking Tesema's battalion, Beshah and Gizachew's battalions from Tegulet and Menz would encircle the Italians from behind and win the battle. If the Italians tried to penetrate Tegulet by attacking Beshah's Battalion, then Gizachew's and Tesema's Battalions would encircle the enemy from the rear and defeat them. This tactic was very effective and the Italians encircled in the major towns and cities were vulnerable.

The preparations taking place in Commander Beshah's camp were of the general kind that had been going on for about a year, but as newcomers, Meseret and Mahlet were highly impressed by it all.

Commander Beshah led the way on his white horse. The soldiers marched behind him. They moved forward, concentrating their gaze ahead without turning left or right. Their thin strong legs were lined with strong muscles and they wore sandals on their feet. Meseret saw how they crashed their feet into the soil and how the pebbles flew up around them, and she sensed the rage burning in their hearts. There was no tomorrow in their lives. Today they would kill or be killed. Most of the soldiers did not appear to notice the newly arrived girls. One soldier smiled at them and they smiled back.

"He is a good man. Don't you think so?"

"Yes. Let's try to reach uncle Beshah," said Meseret, changing the topic.

When they saluted Commander Beshah, he greeted them casually with rebuke. "What are you doing here?" he said to them, surprised.

"We came to assist you," Meseret answered.

He smiled and looked upon her lovingly. "Thank you. I will meet you later. Go back and wait for me in the village," he commanded, dismissing them as he went galloping away. The girls heard his orders but were not happy with the idea of returning to the village.

Many soldiers passed the girls, pushing them aside without noticing who they were. "You girls join with us without carrying a rifle. Good for you," the soldier who smiled to them earlier teased them as he passed by them.

[26]

Meseret and Mahlet joined with the women and the non-militias who followed the soldiers from afar. The soldiers moved along the plain that stretched from Sasit to Tamra-Ber to preserve energy and to camouflage themselves from the enemy. After four hours, the advance unit of the Ethiopian battalion reached the junction at Addis Ababa-Asmara main route in Tamra Ber. The advance unit took cover and waited silently.

The Italian army reached Tamra-Ber and turned left in the direction of Sela Dingay. The Beshah's battalion did not fire a shot; they were waiting for the command. They knew that the command to fire would come when the enemy was so close that they could identify the black spots in the enemy's eyes.

At the right time, a hail of bullets began to fly; many Italians fell. Two trucks caught fire and a third one was overturned. Another car went down a hill with the soldiers flying out of the truck. The Italians fought ferociously, taking defensive positions. They started shelling the partisan positions with artillery guns.

Meseret began to run to the partisans, unaware of the risk of such action. She entered the battlefield and felt a new urge to run. She heard artillery fire, causing her to stop, then continued running as if nothing had happened.

"Meseret wait for me. Where are you running to?" cried Mahlet following her, her large frame weighing on her every move.

The sound of the machineguns, the rifles firing and the artilleries shelling seemed as if it was ushering the Judgment Day. An artillery shell fell not far from Meseret and Mahlet. The two girls fell on the ground and kept quiet. They did not even notice when the smiling soldier came to them, laying low and telling them that they should follow him and imitate his movement. He touched Meseret's hands and smilingly told her to follow him. "You should not stand but crawl like this," he said still crawling forward. The girls' dresses made crawling difficult. "You should have worn trousers like us, not dresses, gallant fighters of Ethiopia," he joked.

They reached the fire line and took a position. "Don't run, move or stand up. Keep your heads down and watch the fighting," the smiling soldier instructed them and returned to firing at the enemy.

"Continue the pursuit of the enemy a little bit further," commanded Beshah, as if he had read the wishes of his soldiers.

Meseret looked at her uncle from afar. She could observe only his face. It had darkened and his eyes were glowing red like fire. She had never thought of this short, stuttering, and smiling uncle of hers as a fierce fighter. She felt the change that the battle had brought about him. As she watched him through the smoke, dust, and chemicals that filled the air, she saw him as a giant in spirit and body.

Awakened from her thoughts by a horrendous voice audible from afar, Meseret turned her gaze in bewilderment. A large army was marching towards her. She turned and looked towards the soldiers commanded by Beshah. They did not seem to have noticed. For the past few days, she had been the victim of a dreadful recurring dream in which she was faced with a harrowing situation and tried to cry out for help, but nothing came of it. She cried but no voice came out of her throat. That same gripping feeling was choking her now. She wanted to tell them that the enemy was approaching from behind, but the shock of fear overwhelmed her attempt to warn her companions.

"Our friends are approaching," said the smiling soldier, as if to relieve her from her overpowering fears.

"Is that so?" said Meseret and turned her face to the approaching friends. She identified the famous Commander Gizachew Haile without anyone pointing him out to her. His Afro hairstyle was impressive. His movements were agile and he carried his machine-gun as if it was a rifle.

Meseret remembered the story she had heard in Nib Washa about the legendary Gizachew Haile. He was district governor in the frontier lands. Rumor had it that long ago he had been disappointed with the provincial governor and in defiance became a bandit. After the Italians invaded Ethiopia, he was granted amnesty, he then went to the northern front to fight the enemy, where he had fought bravely in the first months of the battles in Tigrai before being wounded. At the end of the battle, as he lay on the ground wounded, he had called his militia and his servants and ordered them to raise their hands and touch the sky. His servants asked him how that would be possible. To which he replied, 'Then Menz is far away as the sky. Do not think that you will reach Menz alive if the battle is lost. Fight it out with every last drop of your blood.' Seeing him now, Meseret was impressed with his metaphor of raising a hand to touch the sky.

"Commander Tesema has entered the war from the back," announced a voice. Meseret saw Tesema and his brother Istefo together. The first was easily identifiable by his protruding teeth and the second by his baldness.

The battle intensified, and it was as if the presence of this agile commander, Tesema Irgete, galvanized the troops and drove away their fatigue.

Meseret raised her head and tried to look up the escarpment. She tried to identify Commander Tesema Irgete amongst his multitude of soldiers. She had known Tesema Irgete since she was a child. Tesema, with his few, big teeth separated by gaps and awkward behavior, was unforgettable once seen.

The battle continued past the late afternoon and into the early night. The smoke from the fields arose and dispersed into the darkness. Meseret stood up, called out for Mahlet and began to retrace the way she came. She met her uncle later that night. He looked at her as he usually did, with loving eyes filled with admiration. He called her "sister." In this society, where blood relationships were strong, the word sister carried profound sentiments from the heart. "Is your grandmother well and fine?" he asked. When she gave him a positive answer, she detected a sense of relief. "When are you going back to your home?" he asked, trying to read her emotions, while taking care not to hurt her feelings.

She told him that she would never return to her grandmother.

"What about Mahlet, is she also of a similar persuasion?" he asked when he understood Meseret spoke with resolution.

"Mahlet is also determined," she said, and because she wished to end the matter there, she asked him about the battles in Yifat that had taken place earlier.

He kept quiet.

"How was the fighting in Yifat?" she asked him again in a second attempt to steer the topic of discussion. "I heard you fought very well."

"We fought several battles in Yifat. Tesema performed marvelously. Ask him about it, he will tell you all the details. He loves to talk."

"Is it a fact that he torched seventy Italian trucks?"

"Yes, of course. Go and ask him. He will be happy to see you. He is leaving for Yifat tomorrow. I have some urgent matter to attend to," he said and left suddenly.

Meseret went to look for Mahlet. She found Mahlet outside and felt so happy to see her that she kissed her. She told her about her discussion with Commander Beshah. She started to tell her about the detailed discussions but stopped short when she saw the smiling soldier, the one who comforted them on the battlefield.

"I was talking with the soldier who comforted us on the battlefield while you were with uncle Beshah. His name is Sergeant Samuel," said Mahlet pointing to Sergeant Samuel.

"Good evening. You are a brave woman," said the smiling soldier, approaching them.

"Thank you," answered Meseret.

"I am Sergeant Samuel of the Imperial Bodyguard. I am serving under your uncle"

She told him her name.

In the following days, despite everyone's expectations to the contrary, the Italian counter offensive did not come. Sergeant Samuel spent most of his spare time with Meseret and Mahlet. Commander Beshah had seen them talking to one another and thought at first that it was his responsibility to protect them. However, he passed by them as if he had not observed the three of them together.

Later that day, as they were sheltering in a nearby house, Meseret and Mahlet received some trousers sent by Commander Beshah via a messenger. They were delighted by the kind gesture as they felt uncomfortable wearing their dresses after seeing all the other women with the partisans wearing trousers underneath their dresses. Meseret and Mahlet rolled up their dresses, put on their trousers and left the house. Upon seeing the girls, Sergeant Samuel complemented them on their newfound appearance, then proceeded to hand them both a pair of sandals to protect their feet from the rough roads that lay ahead. Meseret and Mahlet appeared dressed with their new apparel in the epiphany festival held two days after the victory in Yifat.

The epiphany celebrations were colorful and encapsulated the unique nature of the Ethiopian Orthodox Church. On the appointed day, holy priests took the tabots, the symbols of the Ark of the Covenant, to the rivers. The rivers symbolize the river of Jordan, where Jesus baptized. The Tabots symbolize the Ark of the Covenant, the communication tent through which God's will is proclaimed. Thus the Old Testament — symbolized by the Ark of the Covenant, and the Baptism of Jesus in Jordan where God's will is proclaimed from heaven, were recreated. The Old and the New Testaments are fused in the unique Ethiopian Orthodox Church pillars of belief. The synagogue where the Ark of the Covenant dwells was renamed the Church of St. Mary of Zion in the era of Christianity. The Mother of Jesus and

Zion in the Ark of the Covenant became synonymous.

Epiphany is also a carnival where youngsters dance and show their jubilation. Men and women dance amidst people standing in circles clapping and singing. For the first time Sergeant Samuel joined the traditional dance with Meseret and Mahlet. Samuel and Meseret were applauded. Samuel also praised Meseret for her dance.

After the carnival, Sergeant Samuel walked to camp with Meseret and Mahlet. Back at camp, they found Commander Beshah exhilarated by the news contained in the letter from his friend General Abebe. The General gave an account of how he had defeated the Italian forces at the Battle of Salayish. Commander Beshah had heard about a big battle fought between the Ethiopian Army under the command of General Abebe and four Italian battalions assisted by airplanes, which had resulted in Ethiopian victory. Now he read the details in the letter written by General Abebe himself. He told Sergeant Samuel, Meseret and Mahlet about the Battle of Salayish when they came in to greet him. Everybody was happy.

The person who brought the letter from General Abebe greeted Samuel and gave him a letter written to him. Samuel read the letter and his ensuing happiness was written all over his face.

"What other good news is the letter carrying?" Mahlet asked Samuel.

"It is a letter from my friends in General Abebe's Western Shewa Army. They are private Hailu and Tewodros. They wrote about the illustrious victory in the Battle of Salayish and

I am happy they are well and doing fine," he said.

The victory at the Battle of Salayish awakened the interest of Meseret; she wished to know more about General Abebe. "Do you know General Abebe in person?" asked Meseret.

"He was our commander in the Imperial Bodyguards. I was a Sergeant in his battalion, though I am not a friend of his. But I know him as the most humane, considerate and humble commander. He addresses private, commissioned and non-commissioned officers under him all as 'gentlemen'. A few years before the war with Italy broke up he was transferred from the Imperial Bodyguards to the Arada Police command."

"Why?" asked Meseret.

"It all started because of his wife, Mrs. Konjit, who is now with him," said Samuel and smiled. General Abebe and Major Mekuria Bantyirgu quarreled over her. General Abebe was transferred as commander to Arada Guards and Mrs. Konjit was put under house arrest."

"What was the lady's crime?" she asked.

"His Majesty does not like palace women and relatives to be the cause of such scandals. Later on, His Majesty wedded her to General Abebe."

Sergeant Samuel told them that General Abebe was the leader of the Army stationed in Northwestern Shewa, like General Kebede leading the army stationed in Yifat, Tegulet and Menz. Samuel also told the girls about the ancestors of General Abebe.

"General Abebe Aregai was the grandson of the legendary General Gobena, who united the Oromos under Menelik II to ward off the European colonizers during the period of the Scramble for Africa. As a devout, church-educated Orthodox Christian, General Gobena believed Ethiopia's territory extended to the Atlantic Ocean in the West and the Indian Ocean in the South. Menelik II had felt confident that he would accomplish this feat with the staunch support of the tens of thousands of armies of the former Emperor Tewodros now gathered around him. With the support of General Gobena and the tens of thousands of Gobana's equestrians army, Emperor Menelik II wrote the European powers proclaiming that Ethiopia's territory extended as far south as Tanganyika, as far east as the Indian Ocean, and as far west as Ghana and Mali and warned them against sending armies to these regions.

Meseret and Mahlet insisted that Samuel tell them what he and his friends were doing in the Imperial Bodyguard when they were in Addis Ababa. He told them that before the invasion of Italians, he was a Sergeant in the Imperial Bodyguard and after Emperor Haile Selassie left for the League of Nations, some soldiers in the Imperial Bodyguard were assigned in different army units. "Hailu and Tewodros were assigned under General Abebe, I was assigned to serve under Commander Beshah and Ahmed, another friend, accompanied the Emperor to Harar."

"Are you happy with your assignment under Commander Beshah?" asked Meseret.

"Very much so, especially these days after I found you two ladies for a companion," he answered, teasing them.

A week after their discussions about the victory of the Battle of Salayish, a letter arrived addressed to Commander Beshah from Commander Tesema requesting assistance. The letter conveyed fifteen days earlier, stated that

900 native Italian soldiers had surrendered to him and were incorporated into his army. He acquired hundreds of modern rifles and several machineguns, which had reinforced his army.

Commander Beshah was exhilarated by the massive desertion of native Italian soldiers. Two years since the beginning of the liberation war, the momentum of the struggle was growing rather than diminishing. An earlier letter written to Commander Beshah from one of the Addis Ababa-based secret agents had explained how the Italians were trying to occupy Harar and that heavy fighting was taking place in Sidama. It also stated that Yirgalem, though subjected to heavy aerial and artillery bombardment with chemicals, poison and flamethrowers was holding ground. It mentioned that the year was fruitful in the diplomatic arena, and that with the Emperor's diplomatic fervor, the League of Nations had condemned Italy, which led the fascist government to withdraw its membership from the League.

Commander Beshah tried to view the defection of the native Eritrean Italian soldiers en masse from a wider perspective. Italy's army, though numerous, was forced to recruit more native soldiers and was bogged down in a seemingly endless war in Ethiopia. Hundred thousands of native Eritrean and Somalis were mobilized from their colonies Eritrea and Italian Somaliland, before and after the invasion of Ethiopia. The Eritrean soldiers were mainly orthodox Christians like the Ethiopians, and they were outraged by the cruel and heinous acts committed by the Italians—the burning of churches, the killing of Kahns and the barbaric execution of priests. They were also disgruntled at being used as cannon fodder, placed in the first line of defense and offense, which led to heavy causalities amongst them. Some of the Eritrean Italian soldiers were also anti-colonialists, like the rest of the colonial people in other parts of Africa and Asia, and therefore sympathized with the fight of the single black nation to preserve its independence.

After two days, another letter followed from Commander Beshah with the information that Commander Tesema had received information that the Italians were to attack Yifat the next day. He asked for the assistance of Commander Beshah immediately.

The defection of 900 Eritrean, Hamasien, native Italian soldiers caused Italy to launch a massive offensive against the army in Yifat. Tesema, confident with his newly gained strength, called on the assistance of Commander Beshah, while neglecting to ask assistance from Gizachew Haile, and failed to inform the situation to the overall commander General Kebede. The action compromised the agreed upon triangular strategic defensive and offensive tactic.

Commander Beshah left for Yifat to provide his assistance as requested by Tesema. Meseret and Mahlet followed the army to Yifat, with the smiling Sergeant Samuel nearby. Meseret and Mahlet, who now had a few months experience on the battlefront, considered themselves as seasoned fighters.

3

When the battalion commanded by Beshah reached Yifat and entered the war in support of Tesema's army, the surrounding areas of Yifat was burning. The Italians, in the vain hope of subjugating the population with terror, had enclosed women, children and the elderly in their huts, and then proceeded to burn them alive. To endanger the survival of the villages the newly cut grain was also burned to the ground.

The Italians had in a swift maneuver controlled the Weja Michael height and started to move towards the church. About fifty partisans ran to be first to occupy the church ground. Many were machinegunned on the way to the church, but some reached the church compound before the Italians. They entrenched themselves in a defensive position on the height and were able to defend the church.

The army, under Commander Beshah entered the battlefield. The Italians encircled on the western side, retreated and were vanquished, losing many rifles to the Ethiopians. Many soldiers died heroically.

Minor partisan leaders from the surrounding areas entered the fighting and the Italians revised their tactics in light of the new situation. The Italians brought in reinforcements from Debre Sina, the nearby town.

The Italians broke the encirclement and retreated to the road from Dessie and Yifat to Tamra-Ber. With this maneuver, the Italians achieved a strategic advantage. They had started a battle that had brought Beshah's army to Yifat, and then closed the exit route to Sasit.

The Ethiopian army was happy with the magnificent victory, which had enabled it to acquire many modern rifles, machineguns and lots of rounds of ammunition.

"That was a magnificent victory," said Commander Beshah when he met Commander Tesema.

"Yes, it was a fantastic victory," said Tesema Irgete, attempting to show his exhilaration by a movement of war dance. He cracked jokes and moved his legs like a dancing man, something he was apt to do when in an excited mood. Tesema saw his brother coming towards him and he called out while pointing to his baldhead, "Congratulations, Istefo, you have preserved your head. I was afraid that it would be a good target."

"Don't you see that your teeth are also a good target?" retorted his brother, jokingly pointing at Tesema's protruding teeth. Their comrades in arms laughed at the wit of the brothers.

After a while, upon Beshah's insistence, Tesema wrote a letter to Commander Gizachew and the overall commander General Kebede about the victory achieved by the battalions in Yifat and Tegulet.

Meseret, in the meantime, went in the direction of the Mosque to say hello to the Sheik, whom she had met with her mother on her first visit to Yifat prior to joining the Ethiopian army. Shortly she met him on the way to the mosque, and when she approached to salute him, he recognized her and smiled. "How could I forget the girl who asked me about the blessed land?" he commented. She was happy that he had not forgotten her. She told him she was on her way to his home to pay her respects. He insisted that they both go to his home for a cup of coffee but she respectfully refused the offer. He told her that he was going to her uncle's camp and on their way to

Commander Beshah's camp, he told her about the victory the patriots in Keffa had won against the Italians. She was joyful at the news. He also told her that he carried a letter from Private Ahmed of the Imperial Bodyguards for Sergeant Samuel."

"Sergeant Samuel will be very pleased to receive the letter. He mentioned Ahmed was a dear friend when he discussed the Battle of Maichew."

When they reach the camp, the lunch festival had already started.

The festival was a joyful occasion. Beshah read the letter from the Keffa patriots. It described how the patriots, by the will of God, had ousted the Italians from all towns except Jimma.

Sergeant Samuel received his private letter from Sergeant Ahmed who was his comrade in the Imperial Bodyguard. Sergeant Samuel was the immediate commander of the then Private Ahmed. He read the letter with delight.

The mention of the name of Harar reminded Meseret and Mahlet of what Samson had told them two years earlier, "If you stand on the cliff near Yifat you could look at Harar," said Mahlet, trying to repeat what Samson told her and Meseret before he left to the northern war front.

"The city will not be visible, but Hararghe is visible," said the Sheikh. "Harar is the third Muslim most holy place in the world," he added.

"Please tell us more," Meseret asked.

The Sheikh told them about the ancient city of Harar. He told them that Harar was an Islamic learning center. He told them how Harar had influenced anti-colonial fighters throughout the Muslim world. He also told them that mosques named after Harar are found in the Ogaden, Somalia up to the Indian Ocean. Meseret and Mahlet were impressed. Whenever Ahmed's name was mentioned, they would remember Harar.

"What is Ahmed doing in Jimma?" asked Meseret

"He left for Harar first and joined General Umer Semeter as a soldier. He was later assigned to assist the patriots in Jimma," answered Samuel, still reading the letter. "He says in his letter that he has written to his friends with General Abebe. He is asking me to congratulate the Gondare on the achievements of his relatives in the frontier lands and in Jimma."

"Who is the Gondare?"

"His name is Tewodros. We call him the Gondare since he is from the town of Gondar," he said and continued reading. "He also asked me to greet the Menze if I ever met him."

"Who is the man from Menz?"

"His name is Hailu. I mentioned him to you earlier"

"Where are they now?".

"They are in Bulga with General Abebe Aregai's army."

4

Before the feast had concluded, the messenger sent to Gizachew Haile returned carrying a letter from Gizachew himself. Gizachew's letter was short and precise. It congratulated them on their victory and pleaded Beshah to return to Tegulet immediately and

Tessema to get ready to give support during the coming battle to defend Sela Dingay. The Italians planned to occupy Sela Dingay the next day and he informed them that he had already moved to Tegulet from Menz. Sela Dingay was a strategic town for Menz, Tegulet, Woreyilu and Yifat. Sela Dingay was the residence of the Egyptian Archbishop of the Orthodox Church before he left for Egypt after the Italians defeated the Emperor's Army. The possibility of the Italians taking over Sela Dingay had very serious implications. Something had to be done immediately to avoid a major catastrophe.

In hindsight, Beshah and Tesema regretted their over-confidence infighting the Italians by themselves, without prior consultation with Commander Gizachew and the Regional commander General Kebede.

Commander Gizachew's letter was direct; it demanded a swift course of action and sacrifices. It stated the need to defend Sela Dingay at any cost. If Sela Dingay fell, then it would not be possible to defend the rural areas of Tegulet, Yifat and Menz. The Italian maneuver of retreating and occupying the main routes from Dessie to Addis Ababa effectively shut the crossing to Sasit and Sela Dingay. The Italian goal was to acquire tactical and strategic advantage over the Ethiopian forces. Commanders from Beshah's and Tesema's battalions met and drew detailed plans to break the encirclement and return to Tegulet.

"We will break the encirclement during this night and we will pass to Tamra-Ber," declared Tesema and suggested that they should break the encirclement with a staccato of machinegun fire and daredevil tactics. Commander Tessema was legendary for conducting successful military operations. In previous times, he was famous for such forceful breakthroughs. The strategy was simple; when he reached a blockade, he would level his machinegun like a rifle and fire it directly through the Italian line like a madman. The Italian soldiers, along with the Libyan and Eritrean bandas and native soldiers had long believed that Tesema had a magic amulet that protected him from bullets, a myth that Tesema welcomed with pride. The planners considered this kind of dramatic breakthrough as dangerous and they preferred to slip away from the enemy quietly in the middle of the night, without firing a shot.

Later in the day Commander Beshah passed by Meseret and Mahlet. He smiled and walked away. Meseret followed him and started to walk beside him. He felt that she wanted to ask him a question; however, they walked in silence. He heard from Samuel that Meseret had predicted from the start that the Italians would try to occupy Sela Dingay when Beshah's army moved to Yifat. He was expecting her to boast about her prediction. On the contrary, she asked him how Gizachew came to know the Italians' intent to occupy Sela Dingay.

"He might have found the information from the secret services. After the last war, in Tamra-Ber, the Italian General wrote an amnesty letter to Gizachew and he rejected the offer. Gizachew suspected that the rejection of the offer might have led the Italians to conduct an offensive, and thus he started to prepare a counteroffensive. General Kebede also agreed with Gizachew's plan. Thus, he might have moved from Menz to Tegulet to get ready for the battle. He might have thought I would be in Tegulet. However, it all happened differently.

"How did Gizachew know for sure that the Italians would try to capture Sela Dingay tomorrow?" she insisted.

"I do not know. Anyway, we will reach Tegulet by tomorrow. Nothing will prevent us."

Meseret kept quiet. He continued on his way, while she returned to her camp.

On her way back to the camp she passed by the mosque. She heard the Sheik preaching. "The Italians, seeking to divide and rule, preached that there are some men superior to others. Most of all they think their race is superior. But, according to our religion, all people are equal before Allah..."Meseret felt that the success of the planned breaking of the encirclement was destined by God.

The breaking of the encirclement took place during the night. The armies regrouped for the assignment. That night, the soldiers started to move in groups for the Dessie-Addis Ababa trade route. Strict orders to keep quiet and not open fire throughout the operation were communicated to all soldiers. There was no moon in the sky, and they began to move in the darkness. Meseret and Mahlet accompanied Samuel.

"Will Commander Gizachew and his army alone stop the Italians from occupying Sela Dingay?" asked Meseret when she met Samuel.

"We will be there to help him," he said as if the breaking of the encirclement was a foregone conclusion.

The night fight to break the blockade was not as spectacular as Meseret had expected it to be. The Ethiopian commanders sneaked without firing a bullet. They rightly thought that a rifle shot at night would pinpoint their whereabouts.

The only machinegun fire heard was from the direction of Tesema's battalion. When he reached the blockade point and faced a group of Italian soldiers in front of him, he clamored, "Open a passage, I am the hero Tesema," and fired his machinegun like a pistol from his hip level. His soldiers did the same, and the Italians dispersed in the belief that they were under attack. Commander Beshah's army did not fire a single bullet, but they broke the encirclement in their assigned direction.

After breaking the encirclement, the two Ethiopian battalions traveled through a riverbed, crossed the main route and headed towards Tamra-Ber. They had broken the encirclement in Yifat. However, Yifat was lost to the Italians in order to defend Sela Dingay. Tesema was not to return to Yifat for a long time.

It was at about nine in the morning after the breakthrough that an equestrian came to Tesema and Beshah and told them that the battle had already started in the outskirts of Sela Dingay, with the battalions of Gizachew on the defensive.

Commanders Beshah's and Tesema's armies moved with a forced march and eventually reached the battlefield to save the day. Gizachew's army was on the verge of defeat.

After the Italian plan was frustrated, the army settled in Tegulet. Gizachew did not return to Menz. Tesema did not return to Yifat. They were sure that another Italian offensive would come soon. During this time, Yifat was completely burned down and overrun by the Italians. Eritrean defectors to the Ethiopian army who were found wounded by Italians were executed. They faced martyrdom heroically.

[45]

The Italians did not restart the offensive for Sela Dingay in the coming months. The soldiers spent their time leisurely. General Kebede transferred his command post from Molale to Sela Dingay in preparation for the defense of the town.

The smiling sergeant Samuel spent his spare time with Meseret and Mahlet. His eyes were shining and his heart was elevated. When alone he sang love songs. In the presence of others, he whistled the silent song of a hopeful heart.

It was during one of these days that Samuel sent three elderly men to ask Commander Beshah for Meseret's hand in marriage. Beshah was the eldest and the closest relative to Meseret. Commander Beshah consulted her grandmother and granted the request.

Despite the challenges, the wedding of Meseret and Samuel took place in a fitting festival. Mahlet served as the bridesmaid. The priest, in Sasit church, blessed the marriage ceremony. All soldiers, along with the public at large, attended the wedding ceremony.

After the wedding, Meseret, Mahlet and Sergeant Samuel decided to go to Nib Washa to express their duties to the ladies' grandmother, Taitu. They asked two weeks' leave and left for Nib Washa.

"Aha, so you married. Please, please sit down," said Taitu, Meseret's grandmother kissing Meseret and Mahlet in turn.

"Give us your blessings," said Samuel.

"I have already blessed you when Commander Beshah sent elders to receive my consent. Please be seated."

After dinner, Meseret and Kejele went out together and strolled. Samuel and Mahlet followed them.

Kejele was very impressed by Sergeant Samuel. "What a marvelous husband my Meseret has? I know his family and they are good people too. His father was with your uncle in my home country twenty years ago. When your uncle, my husband Samson came back here, Samuel's father returned leaving his son, who was a little boy at the time, with his relatives in Addis Ababa and settled in Ilqoya," Kejele commented.

"We are planning to visit Samuel's parents on our way back to Sasist," Meseret told Kejele.

"You must show your respect by visiting his parents. It is only four hours walk from here."

"I have heard many good things about you from Meseret" said Samuel joining Kejele and Meseret.

"Do not forget she is my mother, and do not tell her only you heard good things about her from Meseret," Mahlet said.

"Your marriage is very romantic, like the marriage of Meseret's and Mahlet's grandparents," said Kejele holding the hands of Meseret and Samuel who were standing on her right and left side.

"How did their grandparents get married?" Samuel asked.

"It is supposed to be a secret, but I will tell you," Meseret said. "My grandmother, Taitu, once told us the story when Mahlet and me were small children. The song Mahlet usually sang about flying like a crow or a swan is the song my grandfather wrote and sang to our grandmother."

"It is recently that I understand why it is popular with Mahlet. It is a song by her grandfather. So what's the story behind the song?" Samuel asked.

"Our grandfather and Taitu, our grandmother were very distant relatives. They fell in love. In those times, neighboring families fought continuously, and to strengthen the family ties, marriage between distant relatives was illegal. The two lovers fled to Addis Ababa together on a moonless night. After she gave birth to my mother, he sent elders to ask for the grandmother's hand in marriage. They finally consented, and our grandfather came with her and established himself here. Even the priest excused their holy matrimony, saying that marriage is only forbidden between men and women who relate to the seventh familial relations and that the law which forbids marriage beyond that was only made to strengthen the family before adversaries."

"People of the old times were kind and considerate. They were not like the people of this time," added Kejele, mother of Mahlet. She was impressed by the way Meseret told the story.

"Yes, I agree," commented Samuel.

"How long will you stay here?"

"Up to the date the Italians dare to attack Sela Dingay," he said smiling.

Their stay in Nib Washa was rewarding. The grandmother was happy to meet them and she even officially referred to Mahlet as her grandchild and Kejele as the widow of her son.

5

At the end of the week, a messenger arrived from Commander Beshah. The commander requested that Samuel, Meseret and Mahlet return since they were to leave for Jiru to assist General Abebe Aregai, commander of the West Shewa Ethiopian Army, who was engaged in a fierce battle with the Italians.

"Are they going to leave Tegulet undefended and go to Jiru?" Meseret asked Samuel on their way to Beshah.

"I don't think so. Gizachew Haile, Tesema Irgete and the others will remain behind," Samuel responded.

"What is the reason to appoint my uncle and his army to this assignment?"

"Commander Beshah and General Abebe are intimate friends. He might have thought that it was his duty to be the first to extend a helping hand for his friend in this time of crisis."

"You mean it is a personal affair and not a national duty?"

"I don't mean that. Our main strength against the Italians is that our armies are everywhere and therefore, can encircle the Italians when they try to fight with any one of our groups. So when General Abebe faces the enemy, someone has to be there to help him. Commander Beshah may have volunteered and General Kebede may have simply agreed."

They traveled to Inewari, where General Abebe's army engaged the Italians. The Battle of Inewari had continued since April 18, 1937, when Beshah's battalion reached the outskirts of the battleground. Beshah's battalion walked in a forced march to the battlefront. Artillery bombardment was audible from afar. Ethiopian fired downed an Italian airplane.

"We are just at the back of the Italians," said Commander Beshah. "Let's take a rest. The battle will stop as night falls. In the morning, we will attack the Italians from behind."

The Italians spent the night between General Abebe's army and Commander Beshah's battalion. Before dawn, Samuel woke up Meseret. He was standing with four lemons in his right hand. He extended his hand to give her the four lemons.

"What should I do with them?" asked Meseret, confused with this present from her husband at such a time. An ominous thought of danger entered her mind. When a person going to war gets considerate and softhearted, it is usually a sign that something evil will happen.

"The Italians will use poisonous gas in this battle. It will not be liquid poison, as they are in short supply these days. These days instead they are using only mustard gas from the sky. When that happens, do not stand counter to the wind. The wind will carry it away. However, if the poisonous gas touches you in any way, rub it with the lemon juice. Two of the lemons are for you and the other two are for Mahlet," said Samuel in haste and left her.

Two Italian planes appeared. "Charge and mix with the Italian barbarians in hand-to-hand combat," cried Commander Beshah. "Hurry up. If you don't attack, you will be the target for the airplanes!"

General Abebe ordered the counteroffensive.

The Italians broke and regrouped to foil the encirclement. Beshah's men destroyed the first contingent and passed to the main Italian army defense zone. The Italian army, displaying great valor, broke the encirclement and went out in the eastern direction of the field, at the cost of heavy casualties. The Italian planes sprayed the villages with mustard and phosgene and left.

In the ensuing days, squadrons of airplanes sprayed chemicals and indiscriminately bombarded the surrounding villages. The bombing did not spare a hut or mansion, fire and smoke gushed everywhere. Amazingly, the poisonous gasses and aerial bombardment harmed only a few.

This battle saved the rural areas of Western Shewa from occupation by the Italian Army.

The Ethio-Italian war was still raging for the second year throughout Ethiopia. The Italians occupied one-third of the country, and the Imperial Ethiopian Armies controlled the rest. Fascist Italy's economy was crumbling. Despite a campaign, Italy was not able to attract Italian settlers to Ethiopia.

General Abebe alone in Shewa commanded 10,000 troops.

6

During their two-day stay with the Army commanded by General Abebe, Sergeant Samuel introduced Meseret to his three friends from the Imperial Bodyguards. She had heard about the Gondare Tewodros and the Menze Hailu from the letter sent by Ahmed to Samuel while they were in Yifat. The Gondare Tewodros was a tall person with a serious and courteous personality. The one called Hailu was of middle stature with smooth hair. When he walked, his feet made a quasi-clapping sound that it was distinctive enough for her to know. The other, Tekle was a former bodyguard currently working as an undercover agent assigned in Addis Ababa.

Tekle was an introvert who did not seem to be interested in what was going on around him. His eyes were small and seemed closed. Tekle was the type of person who did not speak unless spoken. As timid and bashful as he may have been, he was equally courteous. His face seemed kind without any mischief. This quality must have been the reason why the Emperor, before leaving to Europe, decided to assign him as head of the underground secret service in Addis Ababa

During the introduction, she was still carrying the two lemons Samuel had given her the day before. He took one of them and asked if she did not like the lemons. She told him she was preserving them for the next day. "Weren't there lemons during the Battle of Maichew? Why didn't the army during the north and southeast battles use lemons to get relief from the poisonous gas?" Meseret asked him.

"Poisonous liquids sprayed from the air and firebombs caused our defeat, not the poisonous gases. They sprayed the chemical on the army, the water wells, the fields, on civilians and the cattle throughout the country. Then they bombarded everything with flamethrowers. The battlefields were littered with corpses and a multitude of wounded and groaning people, cattle, sheep, goats; every living thing was either dead or on the verge of death. Rivers turned red with the blood of the corpses of humans and animals that died in them. They bombarded the dead and the wounded living things with flamethrowers." He seemed to be reliving the scene. He crossed his hands and prayed. He was so angry and so sad that she never raised the issue again.

It took her much tact to change the topic and his mood. His friends also were disturbed. Hailu aimed to change the topic by asking Tekle to tell them what was happening in Addis Ababa.

Tekle started to narrate what the Italians were doing in Addis Ababa. What he said attracted Meseret's interest. Tekle was telling them about the immense change the Italians brought to Addis Ababa. He told them that the landmarks were changed. He told them the destruction using mines of the replica of the Axum Obelisk found in between Menelik II Palace and the Genete Luel Palace of Emperor Haile Selassie.

Samuel and Hailu were shocked. They started to condemn the Italians, and the two men became so agitated that they would have killed any Italians near them. Meseret did not understand what the obelisk was and what made these two men so angry. But the information raised her curiosity.

"What is an Axum Obelisk?" Meseret asked.

"An obelisk is a monument built in memory of big events. It could be a gravestone, or commemorating victory or symbolizing landmarks. The Axum Obelisk is a monument found in a town in the north called Axum. It is about 20/30 feet long, tall and narrow. Axum is also the resting place of the Ark of the Covenant. The Emperor had built a replica of the Axum Obelisk in Addis Ababa, Which the Italians now have reduced to ashes. That is why we are agitated my love." Samuel explained.

"Is that true?" she asked looking at Tekle. He looked at Hailu without answering. Hailu verified it.

All of them kept quiet, angry at the perfidious actions of the Italians. Tekle continued by adding fuel to the fire. "They also removed the monument that stood in front of the post office which depicted the Star of the Ark of the Covenant."

This created another flurry with Samuel, Tewodros and Hailu. At this point, Meseret seemed confused in regards to the topic of discussion. "How did they build the Star of the Ark of the Covenant?" she asked.

No one answered her.

"They also took down Menelik the Second's statue, the one in front of Arada St George's Church and then had the nerve to bury it." Menelik the Second, forty years earlier had defeated the Italians at the Battle of Adwa.

Tekle also told them about the martyred priests and monks. "They are massacring the priests and monks in major monasteries." Tekle paused for a moment.

The Ethiopian Orthodox church's priests and monks believed that their most important objective during wars was to preserve the tabots, which are the replicas of the Ark of the Covenant. They believed this so dearly that they would even display their loyalty to conquerors of their land only to uphold their divine responsibility: protecting the Ark.

The Italians discovered in the last months of their first year of occupation that the Church's alliance was a cover for its committed support for the Ethiopian army. As such, the Italians declared war on the church and tried to raise the Muslims against the Christians. The Italians did not understand, however, that the belief in the holiness of Ethiopia was pre-Christian and pre-Muslim. It was a belief of God's preference for Ethiopia as the resting place of the Ark of the Covenant, before the birth of Christ and Mohammed. This led to the destruction of the replica of the Axum obelisk in Addis Ababa and the removal of the Monument of the Star of the Ark of the

Covenant that stood in front of the Post Office in Arada. The Italians also killed hundreds of monks in St. Tekle Haimanot Monastery in Debre Libanos and looted many churches. The Italian government's divide and conquer policy of aligning with the Muslims against the Orthodox Christians led the Christian Eritrean soldiers to defect to the Ethiopian Army en masse, and culminated in the attempt on the life of General Graziani. Italy, frustrated with the response of the local Muslims and the Native Eritrean militia, started to depend on Native Libyan soldiers, who became notorious for burning and looting churches.

Towns were depopulated. Some left to return to their rural homes to continue the patriotic war, others to restart comfortable lives in the relative security of their tribal communities. The rural areas were suffering from famine and many peasants left their villages to work for the Italians as construction workers for bread. Villages to the left and right sides of the newly built asphalt roads were growing into small towns, with the poor females working in the bars that had newly sprouted along the main roads.

Tekle, as the man who brought the latest news from Addis Ababa, was highly sought after by those interested in knowing about things such as the destroyed obelisk, the monuments of the Star of the Ark of the Covenant and Emperor Menelik Second statue. Later that day, Meseret met Tekle and could not help but ask him about the monuments and the statue. "Why are the Italians interested in destroying the monuments and the statue?"

"They want to break our pride, our spirit. They want to destroy whatever we have achieved before their arrival," he answered, trying to rationalize the fascist way of thinking.

Meseret was not satisfied and thus took the question to the priest in Bulga, whom she has known for a long time. He told her that the Italians destroyed the monuments and the statue because they were the symbol of Ethiopian nationalism. God had chosen Ethiopia as the resting place of the Ark of the Covenant and the Ethiopians, the black people, as His chosen people in the ninth century B.C. He told her that the Ark of the Covenant came from Jerusalem to Ethiopia in the ninth century BC.

"How did they bring it? Who brought it?" she asked him. He told her the story in length.

"As the history of our church explains, the son born from the union of King Solomon and Queen Sheba of Ethiopia went to Jerusalem to visit his father in the 9th century BC. In Jerusalem, he accepted Yahweh as the only God. Solomon assigned him the Kahn Azarias to accompany him to Ethiopia. Azarias and other Kahns, disgruntled with Solomon's idolatry and belief in gods other than Yahweh, consulted Zion in the Ark of the Covenant. She showed a willingness to leave the dwelling place by floating in the air. The Kahn Azarias with the other Kahns carried with them the Ark of the Covenant in secret and left with the Son of King Solomon, Menelik the First, to Ethiopia."

"The Ark of the Covenant arrived in Ethiopia through the sheer will of God. Upon reaching the expansive body of water that is the Red Sea, the people carrying the Ark realized they faced a formidable challenge: just exactly how were they going to carry the Ark of the Covenant across the Red Sea without damaging one of the

Old Testament's most prized possessions? It was at this moment that divine intervention interceded to provide an answer. Zion, in the Ark of the Covenant, created a thunderous sound and the chariot where the Ark settled rose from the ground along with its numerous followers and floated. They proceeded to float on air across the Sea until finally landing in Nubia. From there, the Ark arrived in Lake Tana before eventually reaching its final resting place in Axum. The Ark of the Covenant traversed Africa. It blessed the African continent with its presence."

Meseret was very impressed. She was eager to hear more about the Ark of the Covenant. The priest kept quiet. After a few moments, as if he had read her thoughts, the priest promised to tell her more about the story of the Ark some other day and left to the church bidding her farewell.

She understood in depth what the well-educated priest was preaching in Nib Washa in Saint Mary Church in Jer. She smiled and felt proud. She even appreciated the poems and songs about the holiness of Ethiopia she heard from the traditional musicians.

She told Samuel about her newly acquired knowledge, and he was impressed. He kissed her and he promised her that the Italians would not be able to take away the Ark of the Covenant.

"How can you be so sure?"

"The Ark of the Covenant cannot move from its dwelling place without God's Will. If it wanted to move, it would float and no one could stop it. I do not think God will forsake Ethiopia."

She was happy. On the second day, she met Hailu and asked him about his story. He told her about his life in Addis Ababa. How he served as a soldier under her husband Sergeant Samuel. He also told her how they went to the Battle of Maichew with her husband. He told her how he came to Addis Ababa after the Italians had occupied the country. He told her how he joined General Abebe's army. She intently listened to him. It was a story about the towns and the relationships between ethnic groups that she had never known. It was also a story about the accomplishments of Sergeant Samuel before she met him.

After two days, Samuel and Meseret left with Commander Beshah's battalion to Sela Dingay to prepare for the expected attack by the Italians. It was obvious to everyone that the battle for Sela Dingay loomed like a dark cloud before a storm.

During the journey, Meseret told Mahlet her newfound knowledge of the two monuments and the Ark of the Covenant. Throughout the short lecture, Mahlet seemed piqued, and when Meseret finished, Mahlet asked her a peculiar question.

"How much does it cost?"

"What do you mean?" Meseret said.

"I mean, how much does the Ark of the Covenant cost?"

Meseret became irritated, "Some things are not for sale," she replied and then walked away from Mahlet to join the group traveling with her husband. Mahlet joined other friends.

Meseret joined her husband when an airplane appeared in the sky. Mahlet ran to Meseret and stood beside her and watched the airplane. Suddenly the airplane dropped two men. Meseret and Mahlet held their heads in their hands and started to cry. Then the airplane disappeared.

"May the almighty God rest the soul of our martyrs in peace," said Sergeant Samuel making the sign of the cross across his face and chest.

The patriots thrown from the airplane crashed beyond the hill from where they stood. Meseret lamented loudly turning her face to the place where they died, "Saint Mary, mother of Christ, is there no justice, is there no mercy?"

"Meseret, our enemies call themselves Christians, but they are immoral. Last year I went on a secret assignment to Debre Birhan. I saw the Italians hanging three and four severed heads of patriots around their neck and posing for photographs. I also saw them posing for photographs standing behind piles of the severed heads of patriots and civilians. Their atrocities are innumerable. You have to have the guts to witness all and to stand astute and never surrender."

Meseret's eyes were flowing with tears. She slowly nodded her head, showing Samuel that the lessons had gone down deep into her soul. Hard lessons learned during trying times

To the Abyssinian (Ethiopian) Gamble by David Low, 1935

Part Two: War and Soldiers

Sergeant Samuel, Privates Hailu, Tewodros, Ahmed, Tekle and the Emperor

1

Before he joined Beshah's battalion and married Meseret, Sergeant Samuel of the Imperial Bodyguard, was a veteran of the Battle of Maichew, fought three years earlier. Hailu, Tewodros, and Tekle, whom Samuel introduced to Meseret in General Abebe's camp, were serving under him.

All of them impressed Meseret with their aversion to talking about the chemical attack by the Italian army. The priest had also told her that it would be blasphemous to talk about calamities brought by God for transgressing his orders, and who had first allowed punishment for sins by omission or commission.

Sergeant Samuel commands many soldiers, but he had a special attachment to four of the soldiers. They were loyal, trustworthy, dependable, selfless and disciplined. The Emperor appreciated these qualities of privates Hailu, Tewodros, Ahmed and Tekle during the travel to and back from the Northern battlefronts three years earlier.

Four of them, along with their comrades, Emperor Haile Selassie, the Ethiopian Army and the Ethiopian population in the war areas had walked through hell three years earlier.

The difficulties they faced here in the rural areas seemed slight compared to the havoc witnessed on their travel to Maichew with Emperor Haile Selassie. It was an experience that had changed them forever.

When the Emperor started to go north to deliver the final blow to the Italian Fascist invaders, the Ethiopian main army with the Emperor was sure of victory. Italy's army, with 400,000 personnel, 300 airplanes, 30,000 transport vehicles, and 400 tanks, was halted by the northern Ethiopian armies, led by the governors of the Northern provinces, General Seyoum, General Kassa, General Imru and others, and by the South Eastern Army, led by General Desta. The Italian war machine had been grounded in the rugged mountains of Northern Ethiopia and the deserts of the southeast.

The larger Ethiopian Army led by Emperor Haile Selassie himself started its long journey to the Northern war front.

The 700 kilometers travel to Maichew from Addis Ababa was undertaken on foot, animal-drawn carts and on horse and mule back. The soldiers and militias were still hopeful of victory when they reached Dessie town, having traveled 400 kilometers on foot.

While they were in Dessie, 21 airplanes appeared and started bombing the town. There was no Ethiopian Air Force to counter them, so the Italians dropped their bombs then left. Bombing became a routine act of the enemy after that.

"There must now be an indispensable pause"-The Duce, A cartoon by David Low

While still in Dessie, Emperor Haile Selassie approved a counteroffensive to retaliate against the Italian victories in the Northern provinces. The Ethiopian Christmas counteroffensive was successful, pushing the Italians back and positioning the Ethiopians to push the Italians out of Tigrai and liberate Eritrea.

The Ethiopian Christmas offensive caused alarm not only in Italy but also with the governments of Britain and France. Britain and France were ready to accept Italy's conquests in Ethiopia, rather than the crumbling of the Italian colonies, afraid of the exemplary precedence of the liberation of Eritrea in their colonies. Ethiopia pushed on its plan of crushing the Italians, not only in Ethiopia but also in Eritrea and Italian Somaliland.

Benito Mussolini, sure of imminent defeat, on December 28, 1935, wrote to Marshall Badoglio his commander at the front, as follows: "Given the enemy system of combat, I have authorized your Excellency the use even on a vast scale of any gas and flamethrowers."

The British and French governments sacrificed the League of Nations in their vain hope of not creating precedence for colonized people by allowing Ethiopia to liberate its former provinces, renamed by the enemy as Eritrea and Italian Somaliland. The population in Britain and France condemned their governments for abandoning Ethiopia.

The chemical warfare continued, with the League of Nations turning a blind eye.

The Ethiopian army under General Kassa, the coordinator of the army in the north and General Seyoum, commander of the Tigray province army, which had no protection masks, were sprayed with mustard gas, phosgene and bombarded with flamethrowers(later were known as napalm bombs). The Western Ethiopian Army, led by General Imru, withstood the chemical warfare and crossed the Tekeze River to attack the Italians and liberate Aksum. This was a prelude to the major attack on the Italian base in Eritrea. With the heavy downpour of the poison from numerous airplanes, the commander retreated to Gojjam, with only a few surviving soldiers. The Italians employed agricultural sprayers to disperse the poisonous liquid, thereby eliminating the side effect of drifting gases. They not only sprayed the battlefields and the surrounding areas with chemicals, but also burned them with flamethrowers, killing about half a million soldiers and civilians in the southwestern and northern war fronts.

The Ethiopian army, led by the Emperor, continued its movement to Korem, even if the

Ethiopian Christmas Offensive was unsuccessful. The massive aerial and artillery bombardment of mustard gas, phosgene and flamethrowers showed the futility of launching a new offensive. The Emperor's led army was also subjected to intensive chemical warfare on its way northwards. The survivors capable of walking, who reached Maichew were few compared to the number of dead. The Ethiopians could not fulfill the ceremonial duty of burying the dead. Northern Ethiopia suffered indiscriminate chemical bombardment. Tigrai's lands and its rivers became a horrific scene of blood and decaying corpses of animals, soldiers and civilians.

The Italians defeated the Ethiopian armies led by the governors-general and the Head of State himself, Emperor Haile Selassie.

The fascists watched from the air the last few retreating soldiers, along with hundreds of thousands of non-combatant women who had joined their brothers, fathers and masters to assist in preparing food, fetching water and help the wounded. The Italians encouraged them to continue the retreat during daytime, promising them that Italy would not attack them. The moving non-combatant forces traveled during the day, confident in the peacefulness of the retreat during the first day.

The retreating mass of women and few surviving soldiers continued to move south in their return journey to their villages. As they reached in their hundred thousand to the plain land extending to Lake Ashengai, numerous fascist airplanes passed over and poured poison to Lake Ashengai and they flew back over the mass of retreating people, appearing to prove that they did not intend any harm. The mass of the people reached the vast field near Lake Ashengai.

"Pah! They were uncivilized savages, without ideals" David Low on the Evening Standard Friday April 3, 1936

Then the fascist airplanes started spraying the hundreds of thousand retreating people below them with gases, burning chemicals and bombarded them with firebombs[3]. Some were soldiers, while most were civilian women. The Italian pilots watched the collapsing humanity under them, then flying lower, mowed their dead bodies with machinegun fire. The burning women and men ran into the lake. Those who drank from the lake or entered into it perished. Lake Ashengai was thick with corpses.

---

[3] The 'special liquid' which is poisonous and flammable and which became known after the publishing of this book was explained in footnotes in pages 15 and 16.

The European Red Cross personnel had been told earlier by their governments to retreat to Dessie, hundreds of kilometers away from the battlefields. Only the Emperor, his bodyguards, military commanders and surviving Ethiopians witnessed from afar the war crime perpetrated by the fascists in what they called the 'March of the Iron will.'

The Emperor and his Bodyguard only moved during the night. They moved through horrifying scenes, facing intense hunger and fatigue. Their bravado and search for glory had all but vanished. There were many temptations for defection or escape. However, they remained with their Emperor. Though walking through hell, they strengthened themselves in the knowledge that the enemy would be defeated with God's mercy and their determination. Each of them had to preserve and inflict damage on the enemy before martyrdom. They came to know that each of their contributions would together add up to earth-shaking achievements. They became patriots; they re-affirmed their pride, dedication and their love for their country and their Emperor.

They stopped talking of the atrocities the cowardly enemy had inflicted. They heeded their priests and the Emperor's advice that victory would only be possible when God bestowed mercy on them. They took the inflicted atrocities as a punishment from God and not the work of evil men. The chosen people of God defied chemical warfare. They considered slavish to submit before havoc and accept one's own defeat. The chosen people of God took it only as a punishment for their unwitting transgression of God's commandment. They did not complain about it since that would have been a transgression of God's will, a blasphemous complaint about God's punishment.

Samuel and his friends thought of themselves as dead, resurrected only to inflict harm on the enemy, only to liberate their country. Many people were running randomly at the mention of any aircraft and were petrified when they saw or heard one. The resurrected did not run and or care about death. They preserved themselves in order to kill the enemy and they sacrificed everything to destroy their enemy when the opportunity arose.

When they started to move out of the northern provinces, Samuel and his friends Hailu, Tewodros, Ahmed and others believed that what they saw had happened all over Ethiopia. As they moved over two hundred kilometers south, they saw villages standing erect, people farming. Everything seemed normal as if hell had not been unleashed on earth.

They did not try to lecture the peasants about their experience of walking in hell. They were not interested. They were patriots and knew what was important and what was not important. They had only to do what they believed in, not for reward, not for glory, not for vanity, but as instruments of God's design.

"... ABOVE ALL, MY DEAR LAVAL, WE MUST CONTINUE TO STAND FIRM....."

Three years earlier Emperor Haile Selassie I, Lion of Judah, Protector of the Ark of the Covenant, King of Kings had returned to his capital city from the battlefront leading a mule that carried a tired child called Arefaye Araya, the son of a loyal Hamasien soldier. The capital city Addis Ababa prepared to receive its Emperor. The city people were waiting for him in the northern part of the city and were looking to the hills for his appearance. His people cried seeing their Emperor so humbled. He was protected by a few Imperial Bodyguards who had passed through chemical warfare and been purged by fire and hunger like their leader. Through crying eyes, the Addis Ababa population saw their humbled Emperor, a frail structure, transformed into a legend and a saintly figure. They saw in the Emperor and his bodyguards, now named the Black Lions, a legendary and undefeated army of brave Africans. The foreign residents of the city, except those pro-fascist, saw the fireproof progressive, the only never surrendering the anti-colonial army of the world.

The Imperial Bodyguard, the Black Lions, who returned with the Emperor, was assigned to the new government, established in the South West in Gore, to lead the country after the Emperor would leave to the League of Nations. Some of the Black Lions were assigned to provincial Ethiopian armies. The provincial Ethiopian armies General commanders received instructions to base themselves in the rural areas and limit the Italian movements in the cities.

During such an appointment, Sergeant Samuel was assigned to General Kebede, the coordinator of the armies of Northern Shewa. The private soldiers under him, Hailu and Tewodros, were assigned with Colonel, later General Abebe Aregai. Tekle took the assignment privately from the Emperor to head the secret service, established to work in Addis Ababa after the Italians gained control of it. Private Ahmed went along with the Emperor up to the border of Djibouti and then joined the Ethiopian army there.

When Samuel recalled that assignment of two years earlier, he smiled. He considered himself lucky to have worked with Commander Beshah, for it enabled him to meet his future wife Meseret.

When Hailu and Tewodros left Addis Ababa to accompany Colonel Abebe, they brought Martha, Hailu's sister along with them. Once they had entered Bulga, Merha Bete, it was the first time in a year that they had been able to relax. Martha, Hailu's sister was a good cook. She got an assignment in the logistics section of the army. Although she was very busy, she managed to cater to Hailu and Tewodros.

Daily life became routine and programmed. Every day from Monday to Friday there were military exercises. The former Imperial Bodyguards and the Arada Guards were training the militia for a half-day. The rest of the day was spent on-farm activities to assist the farmers. Colonel Abebe was busy consulting with elders from the communities in Bulga, Merha Bete, Jiru and other localities. He was also coordinating with the secret services in Addis Ababa.

Hailu was assigned as personal bodyguard to Colonel Abebe. Tewodros was assigned as a military trainer.

On Saturday and Sunday, Hailu, Martha and Tewodros went down to the local river to wash and relax. Hailu had taught Martha how to swim in the Adabai River. Tewodros was an accomplished swimmer before coming to Addis Ababa and joining the Imperial Bodyguards. After they finished washing their clothes and spread them to dry, they bathed themselves and swam in a competitive fashion. Tewodros complemented Martha on her swimming technique.

Two months passed in this manner, then one morning an assembly was called. Colonel Abebe announced that there would be a campaign to retake Addis Ababa from the Italians by the armies around the periphery of the city. He informed the soldiers gathered that armies led by General Kassa's three sons, General Balcha, the veteran of the Battle of Adwa (forty years earlier where Italy was defeated by Ethiopia), General Hailemariam Mamo and others would be in the forefront of the campaign.

The next day, the battalion led by Colonel Abebe moved and took its position in the northern entrance to Addis Ababa.

The counteroffensive by the Ethiopian army was a failure, which led to a disorganized retreat. The Italians executed General Kassa sons, Wondwesen, Asfawesen and Abera. Later the veteran General was also killed.

The offensive to retake Addis Ababa achieved international significance, even if many lives were lost. It demonstrated to the international community that the Italian propaganda about an all-out victory was false. It also led the Italians to make a wire fence all around Addis Ababa.

The failure also led to the dismemberment of many army units. Colonel Abebe at this point showed his capacity to reorganize the retreating army into a strong and sustainable fighting force by implementing an unusual and creative approach.

Colonel Abebe presented his idea for the reorganization of the army to the elders of the region. He told them about the need for restructuring the army in such a way that soldiers would farm the land and when necessary, bear arms and fight. The elders were impressed with his ideas. They consulted with the Emperor's representative in Gore and Colonel Abebe's status was raised to General of the Army.

During that year, General Abebe hand-picked a few hundred soldiers, including Hailu and Tewodros, then told all other army members from the surrounding areas to go and farm their land and return to their commanders by Buhe, (August). He ordered them to come back with their leaders to his camp by Meskel, the festival of the finding of the True Cross on September 27. He also allocated land to those who followed him from the rest of Ethiopia and told them to return on Meskel. During the rainy season, the Italians would not be able to attack the rural areas since their artillery and tanks would become stuck in the mud. The rainy seasons were nature-induced periods of ceasefire.

Hailu and Tewodros observed the impressive return of the armies, starting August 21, 1937, with the start of the festival of the Buhe, the bread festival to mark the end of the winter. During Buhe, soldiers went to their unit commander's house dressed in white carrying their rifles. They bowed down to show allegiance, met their unit commanders and broke bread with their commanders.

Thousands of such ceremonies were going on in the first days of Buhe, August. Then after a month, the festival for the Finding of the True Cross proved to be very eventful.

The campfire was prepared and General Abebe sat in front of a tent. The clergy came dressed in colorful attire and carrying elaborate umbrellas. Then from afar, military units emerged, each of them commanding hundreds of soldiers. The two brothers, Teshome and Abebe Shenkute came forward. Each extended their right leg before their left and kneeled while holding their rifle with their right hand. Thousands of their followers did the same. General Abebe signaled for them to rise. He kissed the leaders and bowed in salute to the hundreds of soldiers that followed the Shenkute sons. The air was filled with the sound of war songs, echoing the determination in thousands of voices.

[73]
The soldiers of Merha Bete demonstrating their loyalty to the chief commander followed next. Similar ceremonies continued for the armies from the surrounding areas. General Abebe Aregai's army has assembled. The army, which had been few in numbers during winter, had grown to tens of thousands over the New Year. With the coming of another winter, the cycle would start all over again.

Mussolini to God: "Beware I will take it as an act of war" A cartoon by David Low, 1936

The Meskel festival ended not only colorfully, but also with General Abebe expounding the detail of his military strategy for a sustainable army. Army commanders were called to a meeting presided by General Abebe. General Abebe set the strategic and tactical components of the defensive war that would bind the Italian movement within big cities. To overcome problems of logistics, he explained that the majority of their army members should continue their daily routine, while each of them should assign a few scouts in the strategic passes identified in all parts of Shewa. Whenever an Italian army offensive started anywhere, the scouts were to give a sign and all the army was then to rise in arms, led by its commanders and assist one another. In this way, a sustainable army of ten thousand soldiers could be built, which could be mobilized for any battle. The commanders were impressed, the clergy were jubilant and the peasants found in General Abebe a savior.

The brilliant strategy of General Abebe proved itself not long after. The Italians encroached into the rural areas where they found themselves encircled and trampled.

In October 1937, the Italians gathered a twelve-battalion army and opened the offensive at Salayish, but were repulsed. Impressed with the victory, Hailu and Tewodros wrote about it in a letter to their former commander, Sergeant Samuel and their friend Ahmed in Harar.

Six months after the Battle of Salayish, the Italians launched another offensive. Hailu was the scout assigned when the Italian vanguard appeared. On that day, while his friends were preparing to slaughter an ox for their lunch, Hailu decided to miss the occasion and instead went to pray at a nearby church located on the plateau. He reached the summit with his rifle hanging on his shoulder and began to walk slowly to the church, praying soundlessly as he approached the church. He kissed the outer door of the church before entering. Once inside the church, he bent down on both knees and kissed the ground in reverence. He approached the cross and in ritual fashion, kissed it. He began to pray, focused and completely attached to the Almighty God, unconscious about his surroundings. At last, he spat on his two hands, rubbed his face with them, made the sign of the cross across his face and chest, bowed low to say farewell and went out of the church with a light heart and a refreshed body. Outside, the streets brimmed with frantic activity; people were walking past the church behind their cattle and carrying bundles of their material goods on their backs. Hailu wondered why. He approached a young man and asked him where everyone was going.

"We are running for our lives and taking our cattle to a distant place," said the young man passing him.

"Why?" asked Hailu, hurrying to keep up with the young man.

"The Italians are coming."

"Where are they?" Without saying a word, the young man pointed the way. Hailu attentively looked in the direction the young man had pointed. From the plateau, he searched for movements in the vast field that extended to the horizon. He could not make out a thing.

"Look closely for the Ethiopian bandas led by the traitor Aba-wukaw. The native Eritrean Italian soldiers are dressed in red and they are numerous. They lead in the fore while the Italian army is in the back," said the young man.

Hailu identified the enemy. "I see them," he said, and then proceeded to point his rifle in the direction where his friends were slaughtering the ox. He fired three warning shots in the air. "They will hear the shots and they will come," he thought to himself, thinking about his friends while he prepared defensive positions to hide from the enemy. He found some large stones scattered across the field provided suitable grounds to form a line formation with his friends in defense against the enemy; and the riverbed on the left side could serve as a retreating outlet if things did not go as planned. Most of all, however, he found the fenced walls of the church to be good defensive line. Hailu was contemplating all of these things when his friends finally reached him.

"We heard your rifle shots and also realized the danger because of the fleeing people. We have sent a messenger to Headquarters."

"Let's enter the church compounds and hide from the Italians. When they are near, we will go to those scattered stones and open fire from there. I think that will be a good idea, the rest will be planned and implemented by the Higher Commandants," Hailu suggested.

"Good," said the soldiers unanimously as they moved into the church, kissing the holy ground upon entering and then taking their positions.

"Equestrians are coming," said one of their friends, looking backward.

"It is Balcha and his equestrians."

Balcha ordered the attack before the Italians could take their artillery from their horsebacks. The Italians faced the Ethiopians without preparation. The equestrians confronted the Italians trying to break their formation into two. The Italians were now amidst wild grass and as the equestrians approached the waist-length grass, they dismounted from their horses. Smoke from burning grass and huts filled the air. The yellow flames rose high and then exploded into black smoke.

"They are retreating under smoke cover. Don't give them time to reorganize or dig in."

"Fan out so as not to be covered by the smoke," commanded Balcha.

The fighting continued until two in the afternoon.

At this time, Hailu observed a group of Italian soldiers moving on the left side in the direction of another church.

"They are trying to burn the St. Abo Church. Let some of us run there and prevent them. St. Abo will help us," Hailu cried, and he moved backward and by taking cover by the top of the plateau, ran to Saint Abo Church.

"The Italians have already reached the foot of the hill of Saint Abo Church," said a soldier and followed Hailu.

""Let's move to St. Abo. You may be able to defend this place with your men," said a soldier to Balcha.

"That is a good idea," he said in agreement. The soldiers ran to St. Abo Church and took up positions at the outer stone walls of the church

"Let's turn our attention to the Italians and wait for them to get near before we shoot at them," said Hailu in a commanding voice.

The Italian contingent armies moved up the hill to occupy the church ground. They were confident no one was watching them. They climbed the hill and when they finally reached a few meters from the church, a hail of bullets hit them. They retreated in search of a better defense line. The battle raged on.

"They are retreating."

"I am hearing rifle shots on the hill beyond. They may be retreating so that we may follow them and get encircled," said a soldier.

Hailu called on a militia and ordered him to go to the hill on the ridges and verify the condition." The militia left. The rest of them continued to fire.

"What's up?" asked Hailu in surprise when he saw the militia return so soon.

"On my way, I met a messenger from the Head Quarters and he told me that Commander Beshah's battalion from Tegulet has control of the hill."

Hailu glowed with happiness. He knew that his former commander and friend Samuel would come along with his Commander Beshah. He would meet Sergeant Samuel by tomorrow, God willing.

A replacement unit arrived in the meantime. "The Headquarters has ordered that you soldiers return to camp and take rest since you have been fighting from sunrise to sunset. You must be tired," said the Commander.

They reported to General Abebe Aregai's camp, and left, ordered to go to a nearby village to spend the night. "Gentlemen," said General Abebe Aregai, who addresses his superiors or inferiors equally as "Gentlemen." "The fighting will stop during the night. Rest until sunrise and then take your positions in the morning."

When Hailu and his friends left, they saw Balcha's equestrians going towards General Abebe's camp. They did not travel far when they heard a cry of disgust from equestrians.

"What happened?" inquired General Abebe throwing the end of his cloak over his shoulder.

"Wako is deserting," answered many voices.

Hailu saw a person running in the direction of the Italians rising, white hand-woven scarf tied to the barrel of his rifle.

"Shoot the traitor!" ordered General Abebe.

The soldiers fired, but Wako disappeared in a ditch taking his white cloth out of sight. The soldiers followed him. Nevertheless, he safely passed to the Italian side.

2

"What kind of a person is that fellow Wako?" Hailu asked a soldier who returned from pursuing Wako.

"He is a relative of Colonel Aba Wikaw. We warned General Abebe about Wako's relation to the Colonel, but General Abebe ignored us. He thought that even though he is a relative of the traitor, Colonel Aba Wikaw, he would remain patriotic."

"If you remember, Colonel Aba Wikaw was a loyal servant of Emperor Eyasu. When Eyasu was deposed, the Colonel did everything he could to fight his banishment. However, when Zewditu became queen and the deposer a crown prince, the Colonel was put under house arrest and fired from his governorship. Eventually, the crown prince became the king, and released the Colonel from prison. But during the battle of Maichew he defected to the Italians," said the soldier.

"Ah, I knew I saw him during the fighting, but I thought that was just somebody who resembled him.

"You are from Menz, are you not?" asked the soldier casually.

"How did you know?" asked Hailu in surprise.

"Observing that your hair is as smooth as that of a monkey hair, as well as your bent back and short legs," answered the soldier jokingly.

Hailu laughed heartily, noticing the correctness and wittiness of the man's comment.

That night they were plagued with bad dreams, but still managed to wake up before sunrise. The battle raged for two days.

On the third day, Hailu and his friends walked to their assigned positions to encircle the enemy. They were conscious that the day's fighting would be harsh since the Italians would dig foxholes and use their artillery.

When they reached the battlefield, they were stunned. The Italians and the local traitors who joined the Italians, who are referred to as "bandas" had managed to sneak away. Wako, a banda, may have guided them. He must have taken them through the riverbed, which was the only unguarded place.

The local people, who had become familiar with the practice that the Italians had when they retreated in haste, of burying rifles and bullets along with their killed soldiers, were digging everywhere in the field the Italians had occupied

"Oh God, what are they doing?" Hailu asked.

"Why are the people digging," asked Hailu for the second time in sheer bewilderment.

"They are digging up graves of the Italians."

"Why should they dig up the graves?"

"The Italians have burried rifles and grenades of their dead soldiers along with the corpses."

"Countrymen, it will be enough if you pick only the rifles and bullets, leave the hand grenades, do not touch them. They are unknown types of hand grenades even to us. They may be dangerous!" advised Hailu.

The peasants did not heed his warning.

At 10 o'clock, General Abebe presided over the festival. Commander of the patriotic units and their men began to pass in front of him, telling their exploits in war songs. The Ethiopian army found a large number of rifles and ten pieces of artillery left in haste by the invading Italian army.

Dinner was abundant with the meat of five slaughtered oxen, along with thousands of pieces of bread and injera[1] brought by the surrounding peasants. Everyone ate jubilantly, seasoned with lively conversation. After the feast, the soldiers took rest under the shade of the trees.

Hailu was relaxing with his comrades when he suddenly heard an explosion in a nearby hut. He and his comrades ran to the hut. "What happened?" he asked the first person he met outside the hut.

"A hand grenade exploded and the whole family was killed"

"How did that happen?"

"The boy saw a golden ring on the hand grenade he found in the graves of the Italians. He thought that the ring was made of real gold and tried to cut it out, while sitting near the door of the hut. The hand grenade exploded and he died along with his family," said the person wiping tears from his eyes.

"Who was the family?" asked Hailu sadly.

"It was a hard-working peasant family."

Hailu pounded the ground with his right foot and felt deep sorrow.

General Abebe ordered that all the bombs found at the Italian gravesite be collected and put safely in the field. Grass and dried wood were piled on top of the hand grenades and they were set on fire. The people watched from afar as the bonfire grew bigger and at last the bombs exploded, making a fantastic fireworks display.

A general meeting addressed by General Abebe was convened. He told them that every Ethiopian should know about the victory at the Battle of Inewari. The victory in Inewari illustrated that our God had pardoned our sins and was giving us victory. He informed the gathering that he had decided to send messengers throughout Ethiopia with the task of informing the people about their great victory. This would give morale to patriots everywhere and would be inspiring news for those who were wavering, he concluded.

The General expressed gratitude to Archangel Michael for giving them victory on this day assigned for his commemoration.

The Battle of Inewari was the second major victory in Shewa, after the Battle of Salayish, led by General Abebe after the Battle of Maichew. It was the first battle where an Italian plane was downed by machinegun fire. The Battles of Salayish and Inewari have created legends and heroes in their aftermath. In the Battle of Inewari, the Italians fielded twelve battalions against General Abebe's 10,000.

The Battle of Inewari was also the battle where Sergeant Samuel met Hailu and Tekle after their separation of one and a half year. This was the occasion where Meseret met Tekle, the secret agent, and heard from him about the destroyed monuments and statues in Addis Ababa.

Part 3: Heroes Come to Villages

Meseret, Samuel and Hailu

After the victory celebrations, Samuel and his friends Hailu, Tewodros, Tekle, Meseret and Mahlet sat under a tree and ate their lunch.

Meseret saw the badly wounded soldiers on stretchers ready for transfer to Menz. This was to clear the wounded soldiers from the area before the expected Italian counteroffensive.

"Those two on the stretchers are Major Mesfin and Captain Mengesha of the Imperial Bodyguard," commented Hailu.

Meseret ran to the stretcher still carrying the lemon in her hand. She came to the first stretcher and looked at the seriously wounded soldier's face. The soldier bandaged all over his face was difficult to identify.

"Uncle Mesfin," Meseret sobbed.

"Major Mesfin is over there," the nurse pointed out.

"Let God preserve you. Archangel Michael will preserve his heroes," Meseret said to the wounded soldier, before thanking the nurse and rushing over to Major Mesfin.

Major Mesfin heard someone approaching him, which, as a trained military man, quickly piqued his interest.

Meseret moved to the stretcher next to Mesfin and smiled at him. "Uncle I heard you were wounded. How do you feel?" she said kissing his cheeks.

"I am fine. God bless you. So you have become a member of the Ethiopian Army?"

"Yes. They said you are going to Agermerfia. Please give my greeting to my grandmother. She will be very happy to go there and see you."

"I will try," he said and added, "I heard that you are with Commander Beshah and have married Sergeant Samuel."

"That's correct."

He smiled and kept quiet. She told him that her units were planning to leave that night for Sela Dingay and wished him well. She kissed his cheeks, put the lemon in his hands and left his side with sadness.

Samuel and Meseret said farewell to Tewodros and Hailu. "Hailu, I think your transfer to the Adabai gorge will bring us nearer. You could climb the gorge and travel to Sasit to visit us," commented Sergeant Samuel

"Yes, I will do that," said Hailu and saluted him.

Meseret and her husband Samuel left for Sasit with Beshah's army.

Hailu's responsibility was to coordinate the transfer of the wounded people to Agermerfia. General Abebe came to bid farewell to the wounded compatriots. Hailu saluted General Abebe and stood attentive.

"Where is your birthplace?" asked General Abebe

"It is in Agermerfia, just near the river Adabai."

"That will be an important place if ever the resistance war is forced to divide into small guerrilla units. Nevertheless, for now, we are sending the wounded commanders and my wife to Menz. Your assignment is to take care of them. We will write letters to the country chiefs to give you support. Major Mengesha was your commander before, and you should recognize him as your present commander. You may pass the militia under your command to Tewodros."

Hailu saluted and then left.

By the next day, with several peasants carrying the wounded Major Mesfin Sileshi, Captain Mengesha, General Abebe's wife, Mrs. Konjit, Hailu, and his sister Martha started their journey to Agermerfia in the Adabai gorge.

Tewodros came to say farewell to Hailu and Martha. Hailu and Martha had become close friends since they met three years ago in Addis

Ababa and traveled to General Abebe's camp. Martha was very emotional when she bid him farewell.

After traveling for about an hour, the brother and sister started to talk about their village and their father and siblings. "Our brother Wolde will be happy to see you after all these years," commented Martha.

He kept quiet.

"You used to like him very much, didn't you? Our parents and neighbors used to tell me."

"You were a child when I left for Addis Ababa."

"Why didn't he leave with you for Addis Ababa to be recruited as a soldier?"

"It is a long story. Tekle and I decided to run away from our village. Then I mentioned my decision to Wolde, but he refused to join, telling me we shouldn't run from our birthplace."

"You see he said 'we' instead of 'you' because he liked you," Martha said.

"Yes, you see, I did not get on well with my stepmothers, I was always victimized. But he got on all right with them. I told Wolde my reasons for leaving my birthplace and he told me he would not tell anyone but still refused to join me. Afterward, our relationship cooled, and I became more and more attached to Tekle. When I settled in Addis Ababa, I soon gathered many friends," Hailu said.

"Our father says that the love between brothers diminishes when they live far away from one another because the distance makes it impossible for them to keep in touch with each other."

"It is a correct observation," said Hailu. His childhood memories only seem to surface in brief intervals. He remembered those cruel stepmothers. He also remembered how he learned how to weave, and how his mother was both happy and sad when she found out about her son's newfound skill. She was happy because her son was becoming a self-sufficient man; but at the same time, she was sad because she considered weaving a lowly trade done by men considered to have the evil eye. Hailu's life became easier as he became self-sufficient, except for one reality; there was always something nearby that reminded him of his past suffering: a tree, a smell, a mountain – any number of things he met throughout the day bred a sense of uneasiness in his soul. He hated his home village and decided to run away to Addis Ababa and join the army. Tekle, his friend in the same village was of a similar mind and both of them fled to Addis Ababa. Hailu and Tekle became guards in the Bullet Factory; and not long afterward, they got promotion to Imperial Bodyguard. They were happy to realize their childhood wishes.

"Did you hear the news?" Martha said. "Our elder sister has gone to Geregera."

Out of all of Hailu's siblings—three brothers and two sisters—his eldest sister is the most precious to him. She was like the old woman who fed the prophet Elias during the period of natural calamities. She settled in one place, unlike her itinerant siblings. Her parochial life had proved very convenient for her relatives, they knew that they could find her at hand if they ever needed her help. Hailu's other siblings are more reminiscent of the Bible story of the prodigal son who took his share of the family money only to return and ask them for their forgiveness as a destitute wanderer.

"Where is our youngest sister?" asked Hailu.

"Last time I heard, she was in Tegulet."

Hailu and Martha, immersed in their conversation inadvertently had ignored the peasants carrying the wounded soldiers. One of the peasants asked Hailu whether the farm they saw below belonged to Archbishop Mathewos.

Hailu kept quiet. The farm belonged to his ancestors before it was taken over by unlawful inheritance to the mother of Emperor Menelik II.

"That is Patriarch Mathewos' land, isn't it? By the way, the Patriarch has gone to Egypt," insisted the peasant.

"Is it true?" asked Hailu happy to hear such worthy information.

"It is a fact, is he relative of yours?" asked the peasant wondering about Hailu's intense interest in the news.

"No, the farm used to belong to my forefathers and currently the patriarch owns the lands."

"This makes it clear why you were happy to hear that he returned to his home country Egypt. During this time when there is no government, can you consider not paying his tithes?"

"Maybe," answered Hailu in what seemed a witty joke.

"You might feel confident as General Abebe's man. But who knows?"

Moments later, a lonely man on top of a donkey joined them. He climbed down from the donkey and relieved one of the peasants carrying a stretcher.

"Where are you going?" asked Hailu.

"I am going to my village, which is close by. It is near Nib Washa. What about you?" asked the stranger certain that his motives were pristine enough that no one would arbitrarily bestow harm on him.

"We are going to Agermerfia," said Hailu and told him the name of his father.

"Ah, I remembered that you used to have fiancée Aster, who is my relative, arranged through your father, but later your father paid the ransom and the wedding was canceled."

"Yes" said Hailu, remembering the woman whom he had married for more genuine reasons. Her name was Tiruwork. She was his neighbor in Addis Ababa. Once she asked him to help her to take out barley from the family granary (otherwise known as a gotera).

Tiruwork climbed into the granary, carrying a dish, and Hailu stood near the granary and looked at her bent back as she tried to pick the grain with the cup. He was very impressed. She instinctively felt his eyes on her back. She turned her face and their eyes met. Hailu's eyes went to her breasts, and she sensed the admiration in his eyes. Hailu was afraid to display his emotions. When she handed him the cup, she diffidently, but intentionally, touched his fingers in a flirtatious way, then almost instantly recoiled, as if she had made a mistake.

When they finished taking the grain, she asked him for a helping hand to get out of the granary. Hailu helped her. "Please help me carry the grain to our home," she asked him. Hailu took one of the sacks and followed her.

On the way, Hailu met Tiruwork's mother and stood greeting her, even though he was holding the sack on his shoulder. She thanked him, told him not to stand carrying such a heavyweight and invited him in. The sun was setting, and the hut became dark. Hailu could not see where to put the sack. He was afraid to call Tiruwork and ask her to lead him for reasons he did not know. He moved forward to put the sack on the floor and turned back. He collided with Tiruwork.

"Excuse me! I didn't see you," said Hailu in a whisper. He felt ashamed for talking in a whisper.

"It is alright," she answered in a whisper, holding his hand.

"Goodnight," he said, and he got angry with himself, thinking he should have taken the opportunity to kiss her.

"Tonight we will spend the night together," said Tiruwork. Hailu felt happy. She must be a special woman, he thought, for who has ever known a woman who proposes to a man?

"I will come after mother falls asleep," she added.

"I will wait for you;" he said and put his hand on her shoulder and kissed her.

As promised, she visited him that same night and he embraced her, and touched her full lips. She gave herself to him. He fell in love with her. He asked her mother for her hand and married her. He forgot his bride in the countryside. He began a new life in a new society.

*

The man on the donkey felt uneasy with Hailu's long silence. The man thought he had offended Hailu by his comments.

"Did I make a mistake in raising an old, resolved issue?" asked the man.

"No, no I was not offended. I was lost in thought," commented Hailu, remembering his last day with Tiruwork.

One day, Hailu saw his father in front of his house when he returned from his guard duty. How he would have preferred death than this encounter. He greeted his father but too ashamed to invite him in, stood with him outside.

"I met your wife, she is beautiful," said his father to break the silence.

Tiruwork appeared, informed them that supper was ready and then called them in.

"Why did you come?" asked Hailu.

"It is rumored that our traditional enemies, the Italians, are to invade us. So I came to see you before the battle started," answered his father evasively.

After dinner, the father requested Hailu for a private conversation. Hailu felt uncomfortable, but he could not refuse his father's wish.

"You might have heard that Aster's father has accused me of not living up to my word," said his father. "The Judges declared that I am wrong and too incompetent to control my son. Aster had given birth to a boy from her former husband she separated from two years earlier and I believe that she will bless me with a male grandchild. A wife of yours may not give birth. And I have to live up to my word."

"Father I will pay the necessary amount of money to nullify your contract," said Hailu.

Hailu reached an agreement with his father and provided him the money to pay as ransom and nullify the wedding ceremony.

That night Hailu kissed Tiruwork and said to her, "Please pardon me. I did not tell you that I have a fiancée." He was disturbed when he did not receive an answer from the woman he loved.

"I have reached agreement with father to nullify the wedding. You should not be angry," he said.

"You lied to me," she shouted. Then she cried. Her hands recoiled from his neck and she climbed down from the bed. When he awoke the next morning, he was surprised to see that Tiruwork had left. She had left for good. However, he still remembered her as he had seen her last, young and beautiful. She will not grow old, he thought. Memories never grow old.

"Adabai," Hailu called the river as if it could hear him. Martha came and she too yelled, "Adabai!" She looked at the river hundreds of meters below her with awe and admiration. Their voices echoed back.

The surrounding land breaks into terraced steps of farmlands going down to the riverbed. Agermerfia on the side of the riverbed was Hailu's place of birth and where they stood was the village of the Sergeant Samuel's wife, Meseret.

Five small rivers from different directions join near Agermerfia, Hailu's village, and form the river Adabai. The river flows through a vast riverbed. The powerful river formed a big, thin valley in ancient times. Both sides of the gorge are indented with steps of plateaus where thatched roofs and stonewalled houses clustered around farmlands. The shape of the gorge created a mirage and from the distance where Hailu and Martha were observing it, the river seemed to flow from west to east contrary to its natural movement.

During the summer mornings, the sky above the gorge was misty; but by noon, it would clear up. Magnificent Adabai, just like the sun, rises in the east as big red disc; the moon also appears on the east side of the river mouth. Then the sun and the moon follow each other. The sun disappears onto the western mountain, followed by the moon!

Adabai becomes red with the mud it carried during the winter. Wide and rebellious, covering the dry riverbed; and with a flow so powerful it uproots trees and overturns stones as it continued its seemingly endless journey. During the summer, it becomes clearer, first milky and then blue. Adabai is a river, grand and inspiring in all seasons.

Adabai flows like history, time passing with each drop of water. The people looked at the river as if it were a magical mirror. They saw in the malleability of the river (the overflowing, the rising and subsiding water levels) their collective destiny. They may have seen danger when the river projected a bloodred color or their spirits may have been galvanized when the river displayed a beautiful, opulent tone. The river flows with history, or rather time passes with the flow of the river and history moves forward.

Hailu returned to his birthplace with three wounded people and his sister. He felt as if he had brought a burden and not delight to his childhood village.

Caesar "Bother! The captives are late" Notice 'bankruptcy' on the horse's side. David Low, 1936

Part Four: War, Life and Love Meseret and Samuel

1

Meseret and Sergeant Samuel returned to Sasit from General Abebe's camp in the same day that Hailu reached his birthplace in Adabai Gorge with the wounded soldiers.

Meseret and Samuel found the break in fighting an enjoyable pause. Twice or more, they rode on horseback to Nib Washa and Ilqoya to their parents' homes. Mahlet, less skilled in horse riding, mounted behind Meseret. Mahlet held tightly onto Meseret's waist as the three of them galloped across the wide prairie to visit Meseret's and Mahlet's grandmother. The next day riding on to Samuel's parents' home at Ilqoya and then returning to the camp in Sasit. Samuel was an excellent equestrian and would make his horse dance for the children of the village, much to their delight, and of course, they loved him.

A month passed and for the third time, the battle for Sela Dingay commenced. Sergeant Samuel was busy with military preparations.

The Italian command assembled Italian forces and native recruits from Wollo, Eritrea, Libya, Harar and Addis Ababa for their final offensive. The Italians were so confident that their tactic would work that they boasted about the valor of their native Libyan armies. They even sent messages to the Ethiopian army leaders in Shewa stating that unless the Ethiopian Army in Shewa submitted, it would face not native Eritrean Christians, but Libyans notorious for looting churches, burning houses, and creating mayhem.

The Ethiopian Army battalions in Menz, Tegulet and Yifat took the Italian propaganda about the Libyans as a bluff. No native Italian soldier fought with the Ethiopian army out of a sense of belief, but rather half-halfheartedly. Tekle, the secret agent in Addis Ababa had also sent them the lyrics for the new song by female workers in the traditional pubs in Addis Ababa that ridiculed the Libyan mercenaries.

The quixotic Tripolitania
Has got one hundred Thalers,
He has given me half of it to buy my love;
The fool you will see will give me the rest.
His mother has him cursed,
When he joined the Fascists;
To fight in a foreign land

Some native soldiers tried to show their loyalty to fascist Italians by over-acting. At this time, the Ethiopian army's secret service members in the cities teased them in a similar fashion that seemed to express deep loyalty to fascist ideology. The Libyan soldiers were also subjected to such psychological warfare..."My Sir, I know that there will not be shifta in your country like in ours. Shifta deserves death," says a secret agent to the Libyan in a tone that appeared to express loyalty to fascist Italy.

The Libyan often got angry.

The agents continued to eulogize the fascists, acting like loyal fascist followers. They would express sentiments such as, "Libyans are civilized and will not oppose the enlightened Italian occupation like the ones in Ethiopia."

A Libyan mercenary lose his temper and declare that there was notorious shifta like General Abebe in Libya.

The secret agents made the new information a daily topic when they met the Libyan. After some time he would be recruited as a sympathizer to the Ethiopian cause.

The Italian General Trakia, responsible for the ensuing battle for the occupation of Sela Dingay Town, launched a reconnaissance mission to attain accurate information on the Ethiopian Army's war formation. General Trakia was trying to gather all the Ethiopian armies in one front in order to strategize a way to encircle and defeat them.

The first simulation offensive started on February 23, of the New Year. The Italians tried to break through the Ethiopian army formation around Sela Dingay. The partisans fought bravely and the Italians retreated.

The Ethiopian army battalion, commanded by Beshah and Tesema, thought it had repulsed the third offensive successfully. They were unable to decipher the true Italian motive. On the 28th, of February another simulation offensive was launched and the Italians were able to retreat in good formation. Gizachew's battalion in Menz was called to the front to plan to undertake a counteroffensive.

It was the day after this offensive that the Ethiopian army defending Sela Dingay got information through their secret services in Addis Ababa. The secret communiqué reported that the Italians had brought soldiers from all over the country for their final assault on Sela Dingay, planned to take place at the end of the month. For six days, the Italians fought furiously to break through the Ethiopian's fortification, but to no avail. On the 7th day, the big Italian offensive started.

Tens of thousands of Italian soldiers, supported with airplanes, artillery, and mechanized brigades, moved in a big semi-circle towards the town of Sela Dingay. In this way, they prevented Ethiopian army contingents from moving on the back of the Italians and pushed all of them in a planned encircled position. With Yifat lost to the Italians, the Ethiopian plan to encircle the Italians became impossible.

Beshah and Tesema moved their army units hither and thither to stop the Italians from infiltrating their formation. For the most part, the Ethiopian commanders were not worried about the artillery fires and aerial bombardment. They knew from experience that the artillery fires and bombs could only be harmful if dropped on a congested group of soldiers. Therefore, their strategic formation was designed to obviate risk, so that if they scattered themselves across the vast rolling mountains, there would be a reduced chance of high casualties.

The battle continued into the afternoon. The Italians, through a mechanized contingent, were successfully able to break to Sela Dingay from the Tamra-Ber direction. The mechanized contingent moved fast; they were halfway to Sela Dingay town. The Ethiopian side rearranged their formations so that they could avoid the Italian encirclement.

The Italians were thus able to occupy Sela Dingay. Meseret broke down and cried when she saw the Italian barbarians moving towards the hill where the castle belonging to the grandmother of Menelik II, the hero of the 1896 Battle of Adowa, stood. Systematically, they fortified themselves on the height of Sela Dingay, burning churches and houses, and killing any priest or youth they could find.

The Ethiopian army's two-pronged formation came together bypassing the Italian encirclement, taking its position on the left side of Sela Dingay. Unfortunately for the Ethiopian army, they could not dislodge the Italians from Sela Dingay. Not long ago, Yifat had been lost to the Italians; with the fall of Sela Dingay to the Italians, the rural areas of Tegulet and Menz would be difficult to defend. On the morrow, war songs and commiseration over the loss of Sela Dingay resounded. The poems called partisans from all over the country to come to Sela Dingay and reclaim their rightful land.

Tell people in Merha Bete, Jiru and Bulga;
Call louder so they can hear.
Tell people in Adabai,

Call louder so they can hear;
Tell people in Debib,
Call louder so they can hear;
I know they will hurry and come,
If our message has reached.
Tell them Sela Dingay has been surrendered;
Call louder so they can hear.

The emotions of the people were a mixture of pride and remorse, accompanied with the rhythms of war songs. Meetings between commanders thoroughly analyzed the situation. The leaders were aware that the peasant soldiers would turn to their farming since the autumn rains had started. Therefore, they decided to leave Tegulet for Menz and only operate clandestine sabotage in Tegulet and Yifat. This was the last major battle in Yifat, Tegulet and Menz, led by the overall commander General Kebede and the battalion commanders, Gizachew, Beshah and Tesema.

Meseret was dumbfounded. The black clouds carrying the autumn rains covered the sky. She looked at the earth, took a grass blade and then in a distrait manner, twirled it in-between her index finger and thumb. After about five minutes of brooding, Meseret looked down at the ground beneath her, and in a display of sorrow, folded her hands over her breast.

2

General Kebede, an appointee by the Emperor to lead the army to defend Menz, Tegulet and Yifat against the Italians, felt threatened by the capture of Yifat and then Sela Dingay town; he felt he would not be able to defend his headquarters in Molale in Menz. At the same time, the Italians, aware of their strategic superiority, opened negotiation with him. General Kebede, while negotiating with the Italians secretly through his wife living in Addis Ababa, called the assembly of chiefs and elders from Menz, Tegulet and Yifat.

In the meeting, he tried to explain to the chiefs and elders the significance of the fall of Sela Dingay town in the defense of Tegulet and Menz. He then recalled what happened three years earlier during the counteroffensive led by General Kassa's sons Abera and Wondwesen to capture Addis Ababa and annihilate the Italians. He reminded them that the counteroffensive to capture Addis Ababa ended with a humiliating defeat. He tried to criticize the Ethiopian army leaders in Western Shewa for trying to recapture Addis Ababa. This seemed to dissatisfy the chiefs and elders. Thus, he added that if the General Kassa sons had avoided that battle, the Italians' demise would have been more attainable. At this moment, an elder person rose and spoke.

"The Emperor appointed your Excellency to keep the Italians within the cities and foil their trial to control the rural areas. You have been successful up to now. There is no need to raise the issue of General Kassa's sons. They fought bravely and they were martyred. General Abebe has replaced them, he has kept the Italians pinned to the cities, and nothing has changed. Your Excellency I do not think has a different view."

This assertion needed a wise response. "I am saying just that," said the General. He then told them that with the fall of Sela Dingay, the conventional war would not be possible and guerrilla tactics would be the only alternative. He said the strategy required the organization of the three battalions into smaller groups to conduct hit -and-run confrontations.

"What about your bodyguards and the battalion commanded by yourself?" asked another elderly person from the floor. "Would they be reorganized into smaller units?"

The General continued his speech without answering the elder.

The chiefs and the elders were neither satisfied nor clear about what the General was proposing and asked for the postponement of the meeting.

During the night, the General called a meeting with the most prominent elderly persons. Over dinner, he assured them that he would support the battalions discreetly if they agreed to conduct guerrilla warfare rather than conventional wars. In return, he asked them to order Gizachew, Tesema and Beshah to ceasefire against the Italians for four months. After nightlong discussions, the General, the chosen chiefs and elders reached a compromise. Gizachew, Tessema and Beshah would get prepared, to their best ability, for a counteroffensive during the four months of ceasefire.

General Kebede promised to hand over his camp at Molale to the Italians when they were ready, while his bodyguards and the battalion under his direct command went to Sela Dingay, and surrendered to the Italians. The Italians brought a car to take him to Debre Birhan then to Addis Ababa.

General Abebe Aregai of Jiru, Merha Bete and Bulga, General Hailemariam Mamo of Adama, Southern Shewa and many more others condemned the move. The commanders of Menz, Yifat and Tegulet battalions Gizachew, Tesema and Beshah declared their support for General Abebe and the other Generals who opposed the treachery of General Kebede.

With the defection of General Kebede, General Abebe became the commander of Western and northern Shewa armies.

Meseret was with commander Beshah when Gizachew Haile had entered and said in agitation, "This old bastard has defected," referring to General Kebede. "His wife wrote him a letter from Addis Ababa. She is the one who convinced him. The traitor used his old age as an excuse. It is a lame excuse. He was convinced by his wife's letter and by our current defeat and loss of Sela Dingay. Well, I will meet you later on. Let me rest a while and think about it calmly," he said and left.

"That will be nice," said Beshah

"What is the matter uncle?" Meseret asked

"Well, Meseret, General Kebede Mengesha decided to hand himself to the Italians, and as a result, Gizachew is offended."

"Why?"

"He said that the struggle is entering a guerrilla stage, it would be inconvenient for us to transport such an old man from place to place."

"But that will break the morale of the fighters,"

"Yes."

"Why didn't you prevent him from going?"

"Well, he is better armed than we are. And secondly, this country is his birthplace; therefore we cannot harm him without raising the indignation of his relatives."

"So?"

"We decided that he should leave peacefully. He has already left."

Suddenly, they heard a war song coming from the distance. They stepped outside. Kefelew and his men were coming, all carrying rifles and singing war songs. Kefelew carried a machinegun. Meseret did not know that Kefelew owned a machinegun. Her uncle Beshah looked at her and seemed to fathom her thoughts.

"General Kebede might have awarded it to him," explained commander Beshah.

"Is it to create division amongst you?" Meseret asked him.

"Oh no, It is just to create a favorable impression of him in some of us."

"Is it different?"

"Somewhat," said Beshah and smiled at Kefelew when he came near. "Did you take it from him?" whispered Beshah.

"No. I showed him the way up to Sela Dingay. I saw the cars waiting for him. I approached him and said good-bye then asked him, "Your honor, all these machineguns are going to be handed to the Italians. Why don't you give one to me?"

"What was his response?"

"He ordered his servant to give me one. This is it," Kefelew showed him his new property. "Where is Gizachew?"

"He is at home. He is tired and may be sick."

"Then I will wait..." said Kefelew in a tone that was devoid of emotion, looking at the mountaintops that had darkened with the setting of the sun.

During dinner, Gizachew was noticeably impressed with Kefelew's machinegun. However, before they separated for bed, Gizachew declared that by the next day he would leave for Jiru to join General Abebe Aregai. They asked him his reasons for doing so.

"General Abebe is leading the most powerful, well-integrated and elite military, and he has not submitted to the Italians. Are you going to stay here?" asked Gizachew addressing Beshah.

"No, I will retreat to Sasit. Tesema may stay with me or with Kefelew in Menz," Beshah answered.

Commander Tesema, after the fall of Yifat, had become dependent on his army and on the territories administered by Commander Beshah and Gizachew Haile. His following was also dwindling. That was why Commander Beshah suggested that Commander Tesema stays with him or with Kefelew.

They spent the night in an agitated and confused state. When Meseret arose in the morning, Samuel was not around. She became aware that the elders from Menz, Yifat and Tegulet were in a meeting with the army commanders.

Meseret sat near the door and waited for Samuel to come from the meeting. She felt sad but she did not try to come up with solutions for the tragic submission of the General to the Italians. She remained in sad contemplation for what seemed like a long time. Then, Meseret heard Samuel's voice coming from the meeting. He was carrying a small girl on his shoulder, teasing her to stretch her arms out and touch the sky. It reminded Meseret of Gizachew Haile because of his famous saying about touching the sky.

"How did you come so soon?" Meseret asked.

"I couldn't stay long without you," Samuel joked.

"How was the meeting?"

He briefed her about the meeting of the elders. He told her that when Gizachew Haile decided to go to Jiru to join General Abebe Aregai, elder men of Menz assembled and called him back.

"Why?"

"They asked him why he was leaving them and going to Jiru. He answered that General Abebe Aregai is the only one who has not submitted to the Italians, and he wanted to join forces with him and continue the fight for his country and religion in Jiru."

"What did the assembly say?"

"They told him that even though General Kebede appointed him, they, as elders of Menz, Tegulet and Yifat have renewed his appointment as their leader. They censored him for his behavior. They then elected him as their protector and leader of the partisan forces. They elected Kefelew as his second."

"Interesting," Meseret said.

"The elders also renewed the appointment of Beshah and Tesema as protectors of Tegulet and Yifat and commanders of the battalions from Tegulet and Yifat."

"Where is my uncle Beshah?"

"He has been convinced to move to Menz with Gizachew. We have to follow him. I came to collect you."

Gizachew, Beshah and Tesema implemented a strategy, which incorporated both conventional and guerilla 'hit-and-run' tactics. Guerilla units were encouraged outside the army.

Under Gizachew's leadership, the northern Shewa army declared its loyalty to the famous General Abebe Aregai of Jiru, Merha Bete and Bulga. Thus, in Shewa emerged an incongruous situation where General Abebe continued the conventional warfare, while in Menz, Yifat, and Tegulet, a mixture of conventional and guerrilla warfare strategies had commenced.

Meseret stood beside Samuel and caressed his long hair. In memory of the heroic and fierce Biblical hero, Samson, the Ethiopian soldiers and partisans had vowed not to cut their hair until their country regained its independence.

When Meseret finally arrived in Sasit with her husband, she saw not only her uncle, but also Gizachew, Tesema and Kefelew together. They were preparing to go to Menz.

"Why are we going to Menz?" Meseret asked Sergeant Samuel.

"Maybe for reasons that make more sense to the leaders," answered her husband. She smiled. She stopped probing for information.

3

The autumn rains had started, nourishing the dry soil, scourged by the long, hot summer. Meseret and Mahlet put their hand-woven scarves around their heads and shoulders and walked in the rain. The smell of soil pervaded the air. "Our country smells good," Meseret commented.

Meseret, Mahlet and two other women left the main lane and took a shortcut. They hurried and reached Beshah, who was with Gizachew and Tesema leading the partisans. When the women approached Beshah, Meseret greeted him and forwarded an idea.

"Uncle, let us women go before you and help the village people prepare lunch."

"As you wish," he said with brightened eyes. Meseret and the women passed through another shortcut, disappeared into the valley, and reemerged at the foot of the next mountain. In the elevated country, mountains and valleys were seemingly endless. They climbed the mountain.

The women settled to rest when they reached the peak of the mountain. They looked down and saw that the men were beginning to climb.

Meseret faintly heard a song that seemed to come from somewhere in the distance. "... Call louder so they can hear you," she deciphered the faintly heard song. She heard the war song yesterday. The green, gold and red striped national flag, which the men carried on their way up the mountain, seemed to flap in rhythm with the song. "How beautiful," Meseret thought to herself.

The Imperial flag, which went to Maichew with the Emperor and handed over to the government leaders in Gore, Ilibabor, had come to Bulga two years ago. Samuel had told Meseret about the flag before she saw it. He also showed it to her when they were in Bulga. When the Italians overran the Ethiopian Government in Gore, the Hamasiens, with General Imru, took the flag and preserved it. After one hundred and forty-nine of them were martyred, the only remaining survivor brought it to Bulga and delivered it to General Abebe.

The women descended the mountain gorge to the Mofer Wouha River. They crossed the river, entered Menz and began to climb the other side of the mountain.

The partisans reached their assigned village at four in the evening.

During the night, partisan leaders began to discuss strategy and tactics. Meseret brought them home-brewed beer and remained in the room to serve them. The topic of their discussion caught her interest.

"It doesn't mean that we have been weakened and the Italians made stronger," Gizachew Haile said. "Take the case of Tesema. Tesema retreated from Yifat and continued his struggle in Tegulet. Tesema and his men did not submit to the invaders, nor have the invaders been victorious in Ethiopia. Earlier we had left Tegulet and came to Menz. That does not mean we are at a strategic disadvantage, or that the fascist Italians wish of occupying Ethiopia has been realized," he declared.

"We are not at a strategic disadvantage, I agree with that. But if we don't try to trench the Italians in Tegulet, we may get ousted from Menz within a short time," one of the partisan interjected.

"That is a correct analysis. We should be able to hold the Italians by quarantining them in the town. Otherwise, they may overrun all of Tegulet and pass to this very place."

"In principle, I will take that to be correct. However, we must be realistic. The autumn rains have started and the peasants are concentrating on their farms. They will not come to our aid with their rifles if we face a stalemate," suggested one of the partisan leaders.

A heated debate ensued. However, there was a lot of talking and very little listening. Several people were talking simultaneously. The debate became so congested that Meseret could not understand the necessity for the discussion. A game of politics was going on. The minor leaders supported every idea their superiors put forward, not wanting to risk their positions by exerting a contrary statement from that of their masters.

Finally, the debate settled on the decision that partisan leaders were to return to their assigned places in the districts of Menz and try to recruit more partisans in preparation for an onslaught against the Italians occupying Sela Dingay after the rains stopped.

"Friends, we have to be vigilant and must hurry to the aid of our comrades when one of us is in trouble. We must also send messages orally or through calls across the mountains," ordered Gizachew. In the following days, Meseret went with Beshah and Tesema's constituents to Dengezie. Gizachew went to Molale. Meseret sensed that Tesema and Beshah had begun to feel alienated from the people who had originally elected them as leaders.

Two months passed without any encounter. This lull in the war led the Italians to believe the earnestness of General Kebede's submission and the pacification of the areas under his command. The Italians focused their attention on the powerful segment of the Ethiopian army led General Abebe Aregai.

Meseret increasingly came to enjoy the spectacular landscape of her country; it appeared to her as a chain of mountains. One huge mountain seemed fragmented into many smaller mountains by the rivers that had carved deep valleys all over it. In such a place, a person standing at the top of a mountain could audibly transmit a message to a man on the mountain in front of him. Through a chain process, messages reach every single mountain. The villagers might use this effective traditional long-distance communication system to announce the death of a person to his or her relatives living on the adjacent mountaintop. A loud subsequent echo would reverberate through all of the nearby mountains announcing the name of the deceased person.

Meseret was sitting under a tree when she heard voices echoing like a herald of angels from the Revelation of St. John.

She arose and hurried to the hut in an attempt to find Samuel. Instead, she saw Mahlet frantically dressing.

"Meseret, hurry up and put on your trousers," she said.

"What's going on?" Meseret replied bewilderedly.

The leaders and the militias rushed to the place where the call was coming as if danger loomed on the horizon.

The Italian offensive to pacify Menz and strengthen their fortification of Sela Dingay had begun immediately after the rainy seasons had ended. The Italians tried to penetrate Menz by crossing the Mofer Wouha River. The whole population took the defense of Menz. The people rose in unison to defend their last bastion of survival from the Italian fascists.

The partisans went down to the Mofer Wouha River on the other side of the escarpment.

"You are a great sister, it may be heavy for you, but with your strength, you could crush the barbarians," Samuel said, referring to a big stick a female peasant was carrying to fight the Italians. "I know you will kill a barbarian with that stick and take away his rifle," he added.

She was not inclined to joke. She said simply "amen".

As Beshah's army descended down to the river, a message was being transmitted from one mountain top to another. The call was audible even on Imweta's mountaintop. Beshah smiled. All over, the chain of mountain calls were being sent and being received.

All of the partisans rushed in the direction from which the call emanated, Imweta, which is at the peak of the mountain adjacent to Mofer Wouha River. The partisans in Imweta immediately began to descend the gorge the moment they heard the call for help. Led by Gizachew, Beshah, and Tesema Irgete and accompanied by thousands of peasants and villagers armed with sticks and stones, they were valiantly ready to defend their country.

Meseret moved down the valley with the male partisans. Those attached to Gizachew turned to the left and began a forced march to occupy a strategic position on the left-wing of the valley.

The Italian infantry crossed the river and began to ascend the steep mountain, when its vanguard clashed with the partisans on the last plateau of the mountain.

Meseret hung her rifle on her shoulder and rolled a big stone off the over-hanging precipice as the Italians were attempting to ascend the mountain, then; unable to bear the sight, covered her eyes with both of her hands. A bullet hit a partisan, and he fell down the cliff with his rifle. The partisans opened fire from the front and the left wings, passing and vanquishing the Italian army vanguard.

The Italian army retreated to the riverbed in search of a defensive zone. However, the partisans and the peasants impeded the Italian's tactic by reaching the riverbed before them. A hand-to-hand battle ensued. Groups of peasants circled each fascist soldier.

A woman hurled a large rock at an Italian soldier, hitting him on the head and causing him to collapse. She then snatched the unconscious soldier's rifle.

The Italian command at Sela Dingay, informed of the precarious situation, ordered his troops to prepare for a counteroffensive to protect the strategic stronghold. The General mobilized the soldiers in the garrison and immediately moved them to the top of the mountain overlooking the river, giving them a vantage point. The general ordered artillery bombardment of the other side of the mountain. The purpose of the artillery bombardment was to make the partisan leaders think twice before climbing the mountain in the direction of Sela Dingay, and to give cover for the retreating Italian soldiers. He sent infantry troops down the mountain to assist the retreating soldiers.

The fight continued till sunset. Shortly thereafter, both sides assessed the results of the battle. The Italians discovered that they had lost hundreds of machineguns and rifles, while the Ethiopians tallied their war booty. In an attempt to maximize the profitability of their newfound weaponry, the partisans ordered the peasants to hand over any machineguns they had collected from the Italians, permitting them to keep the rifles they had looted. Partisans who looted two or more rifles used the extra rifles to recruit more partisans. Thus, the Ethiopian partisans grew stronger as their enemy grew weaker.

A number of bandas had been captured, but no Ethiopian had been taken prisoner. It was now two years since the fascist dictator Benito Mussolini wrote to Graziani authorizing him to conduct a policy of terror and extermination of the rebels and the complicit population and to kill all patriots taken prisoner. The local bandas captured were released after being lectured on the virtue of fighting the enemy.

The Italian General moved his soldiers back to Sela Dingay that night to strengthen the fortification of his most precious stronghold. Meanwhile, the Italians were unwilling to accept an honest defeat. They believed they had been setup. Moreover, in an attempt to find a scapegoat for their humiliating loss, the Italians falsely blamed the only ones who had the opportunity and motive to beguile them, the Ethiopian traitors. The defectors were subsequently shot.

"I hope, that we liberate Yifat," Tesema Irgete put forward his view lightly, dancing in jubilation after the remarkable victory. He was testing the feelings of his compatriots. When he received no answer, he felt a little bit sad. Then he saw a tall and shy peasant carrying a rifle that he captured from the Italians. Tesema, perhaps because of unrestrained emotion, uttered an untactful comment towards the peasant, "Look at this clumsy fellow walking like a camel from the desert."

The peasant felt offended by this cruel joke, but out of due consideration for Tesema Irgete's honor, he did not answer.

"Tesema, please don't offend your soldiers or the laymen again. These trying times require from us a fair treatment of the people. We must not act as their masters," advised Gizachew.

"What will they do if they are offended?"

Gizachew kept silent; Meseret approached the two men.

Meseret was also worried about Tesema's behavior. She has witnessed many partisans desert Tesema and join other partisans outside of Menz.

"Meseret, it is difficult to know you are a woman with your trousers and coat," Tesema teased.

"Are you serious my relative?" answered Meseret in good humor.

Tesema seemed to detect Meseret's anger so he wanted to comfort her. "I understand your point," said Tesema, "but it is hard to change ones behavior at this age," he lamented. He even added a story that should have been a lesson to him. "I know a story about General Wolde Gebriel that could be a lesson for me and my type," Tesema said in good humor.

"What is it?" Meseret asked, urging him to continue.

"After the General was appointed governor of Bale, he ordered his servants to serve him wine made of honey, which he drank alone. He also ordered them to cook food for only him and his family. In dismay and frustration, the soldiers under General Wolde presented Menelik with a question, "Your Majesty, does your government rest on the shoulders of one man, who drinks with one glass, eats with one mouth, and reproduces as one man?" Menelik immediately understood whom they were complaining about and deposed their commander-general."

The recent victory over the Italians was the partisans' first victory since the Italians captured Sela Dingay. It piqued the guerrilla partisans' confidence but was only temporary.

In the ensuing weeks, the Italians began, in an indiscriminate fashion, bombarding villages throughout Menz and showering them with poison gas. Then the Italian army began its second attempt at occupying Menz.

Bewildered by the incursion, every partisan was unable to help his comrade because of the sheer ferociousness with which the Italians commenced their assault. Eventually, the Italians occupied Molale Town in Menz and fortified it with sacks of pebbles and barbed wire fences.

That night, Meseret despondently looked at the desolated villages. Not one house had its thatched roof intact. Every roof in the village had been set ablaze. Meseret clasped her hands and put them over her chest, then looked towards the sky and cried in silence. The circular stalls of the huts stood covered with black soot, fitting for a day of mourning. The people of Menz spent the night outdoors under the cloak of a star-sprinkled sky, staring blankly at their burning homes.

On the next day, Meseret went to the place where the partisan leaders gathered to announce lunch. They were sitting under a big tree and immersed in a discussion.

"Meseret, let's postpone lunch for a while," said Gizachew.

Meseret continued serving them a local beer (talla) so as to stay near them to hear the topic of their discussion.

"Well," continued Commander Beshah, hesitantly, "at the same time, they have encircled us in all directions around Menz. It may be better for us to retreat before launching our offensive. We agreed earlier to be mobile guerrilla fighters, and we should not act as if we are the same army we were before Sela Dingay fell to the Italians." Beshah's proposal seemed accepted by the leaders.

"Well," Gizachew Haile said. "We left Yifat and we concentrated on Tegulet. The Italians consolidated their positions there and were even able to recruit soldiers among the population. This has posed a formidable challenge to us."

"What will be our choice then?" retorted Tesema. "Either we try to survive so that we can continue the struggle tomorrow, or we should perish and hand over the land with our corpses."

"Well said," said Gizachew impressed with Tesema's unusual cool-headedness. " Most of us have to retreat to Jiru, Merha Bete and Bulga where General Abebe Aregai is still fighting. I will stay here with my soldiers. The rest of you have to go there. I may die here, but my presence in Menz, Tegulet and Yifat as a mobile team leader will make traitors think twice before joining the Italian barbarian invaders. Everything is in the hands of God. God willing, we will be able to rejoin each other in the future." His tone was unwavering and full of conviction.

"Then we will all stay here. We never agreed to leave you in the lurch," Kefelew said.

"Yes" retorted the other partisan leaders.

"This is impossible dear bothers. Military realities should govern us. My order is that all of you go to General Abebe Aregai. I hope you will heed my orders. My stay here is a final decision."

"How can that be?"

"Brothers the rain is coming," Gizachew said, looking at the sky. "When a black cloud hovers over Waseia Mountain, rain is surely on the way. I will go to Dengezie," he said looking in the direction of Dengezie. "In Dengezie, a handful of partisans could defeat the enemy and survive for a long time." Then he began to walk to the nearest house.

Everybody arose in sorrow.

Meseret thought the measure taken by Gizachew was the correct one rather than the idea suggested by her uncle. Nevertheless, her loyalty remained with her uncle. She did not enter the house. Instead, she stood near the black soot-covered outer door. She looked at the fields and saw some cattle. Then the rain began to pour and she ran for shelter.

"What did they decide?" Samuel asked her when they were alone.

"They decided to go to General Abebe Aregai. Gizachew decided to stay here in Menz," she answered.

"How did you take the decision?"

"We will go with my uncle Beshah," Meseret said, obviously taken aback by the question. They stood in silence without looking at each other.

"Meseret come in here, it is lunchtime," Mahlet announced. Meseret and Samuel went into the house in silence.

After lunch, a contested discussion on the advantages and disadvantages of staying in Menz convened. Everybody seemed to be speaking their hearts without due regard to anyone else's suggestions or comments. The discussion continued all through the night.

Beshah stood up, walked over to Gizachew and kissed his heroic friend farewell for what might be the last they would see each other.

Then Beshah ruefully returned to his seat and brooded over his friend. Tesema felt the same way.

It had been three years since the defeat at the Battle of Maichew. The partisans of Tegulet, Menz and Yifat, apart from Gizachew Haile, prepared to retreat to areas firmly controlled by General Abebe Aregai's army in Merha Bete and Bulga.

4

The journey to join General Abebe's army had finally come. At two in the morning, the partisans, under the command of their leaders, started to move west to Adabai. It was a treacherous journey. The narrow lane has become white from the surrounding earth. The soldiers moved in straight lines. They reached a mountainous path so convoluted in its structure that it looked like zigzagged rope. Meseret found the night travel very uncomfortable as she struggled through the complicated path.

"Meseret, follow the white lane. The lane is whiter than the surrounding earth. You will stop stumbling," advised Samuel. Meseret found the advice useful. Mahlet was never too far from Meseret. At last, she asked Meseret, "Will we remain together, nothing separating us from one another?"

"Yes," Meseret replied.

"Will there be anything that will separate us?"

Meseret said "Never" in her heart, but the word could never suffice. It was as if she had suddenly been caught in a bad dream where she could not speak to prevent some horrific tragedy from happening. It was as if faced with a bad omen. She shuddered.

The partisans reached Adabai riverbed before sunrise. They looked across the river and saw the Italian campfires and the blocked path. An assembly of partisan leaders convened to decide the next course of action deliberated on the coming strategies and tactics. The assembly decided to cross the river swimming, while a strong and able contingent provided cover against the lurking Italian army would the best alternative. After the Italians had been contained and the main force safely across the river, the contingent was to retreat and join their fellow comrades on the other side of the mountain.

"Mahlet be sensible. You should cross with the first contingent. I will cross the river with Samuel," Meseret commanded.

"Ok," conciliated Mahlet, and went to her assigned group.

Twenty able-bodied soldiers went near the Italian camp and opened fire. Meseret with the third group began to follow the second batch. Meseret saw Mahlet looking at her from afar and she signaled her to cross the river.

"The main body has already crossed the river. Give them fire cover and pass the river," Samuel commanded the contingent. The third group moved to the assigned pass. Meseret searched for Mahlet in the first group. Then she turned her face to the place they had just been and saw Mahlet dragged by a Somali Banda serving in the Italian army. She rose and ran towards Mahlet, but Samuel quickly restrained her before she could get far, "what are you doing? You will be killed." Samuel shouted.

"They took Mahlet," she lamented. Samuel dragged her to the other side of the river to continue crossing the river.

The partisans eventually broke the Italian encirclement but Mahlet had been taken, prisoner.

The partisan contingent marched to Inewari where General Abebe's camp was established. However, the contingent faced a hurdle when they came nearer to General Abebe's camp. The Italians had encircled the army led by General Abebe. The partisans that came from Tegulet, Yifat and Menz found themselves at the back of the Italian army. When the partisans began their assault, the Italians discovered their encirclement and started to retreat, paying dearly by handing over an easy victory to the partisans, a victory they badly needed.

Only Meseret was gloomy, brooding over the capture of her dear friend and sister. Mahlet was now a prisoner of war. The possibility of never seeing Mahlet again was too much for her waning spirits to bear; she broke down in tears.

The next day, the partisans decided to move with General Abebe Aregai to Gende Beret. However, Kefelew, who was Gizachew's assistant, decided to return to Menz. His friends advised him otherwise, but he insisted.

"Very well my friend, you may," said General Abebe, giving Kefelew permission to return to Menz.

Kefelew began his journey to Menz to meet Gizachew. However, he did not reach Gizachew. An Italian contingent following him and his partisans encircled them at night in a cave, which they had entered to spend the night. General Abebe Aregai came to know of Kefelew's demise while he was in Gende Beret.

Part Five: Patriotism and War
Hailu

1

Hailu entered his childhood village with some people carrying the wounded soldiers and General Abebe's wife Mrs. Konjit. His relatives and neighbors came to greet him joyously. Hailu was pleased to know that the people in his home village knew of the victory in Merha Bete.

Hailu went directly to his aunt's house and asked her if she was willing to accept one of the wounded soldiers as her guest. She complied. He told her that her kind gesture would put her in favor with the partisan and the Emperor when he returned. She gave her consent. He then left to go to his uncle, leaving the wounded partisans under the care of the surrounding villages.

"Hailu, do you think we can survive the Italian onslaught until the Emperor returns?" asked a villager.

"Yes, the Emperor will soon return with armies from the League of Nations."

Hailu took a moment to reminisce on his childhood, wondering where all the years had gone. Nevertheless, as quickly as he fell into a reverie of nostalgia, he snapped out of it. He remembered that his assignment did not end with looking after the wounded commanders. He had an obligation to mobilize the village people for the cause of liberation.

"Wolde, do you know that I have failed General Abebe," Hailu said.

"In what way," asked Wolde.

"I was not able to recruit even one partisan for the struggle. The day after tomorrow I have to go to him and report."

"You may count me as one of your recruits."

Hailu felt thrilled, "As you wish," agreed Hailu.

During the commemoration day of Saint George, people from the village visited Hailu at his home. The first to arrive were the children with their sticks on their shoulders, then the elderly with their rifles. At last, the family priest arrived with his rifle hanging from his shoulder while holding a cross in his right hand.

"Good afternoon Father" Hailu greeted him, walking towards him to show his respect.

The priest presented the cross to Hailu and he kissed it.

"Look, I just bought this rifle. What is your expert opinion of it?" asked the priest.

"It is a very good rifle," Hailu commented. "I thought you had a rifle like this."

"I sold mine five years ago. We priests do not carry rifles during peacetime. It is better not to carry one at all."

"Is it forbidden in our religion?"

"Oh, I forgot my duty," said the priest then entered Hailu's house. Everyone rose.

The priest blessed the bread and then gave it to the guests. Everyone sipped local beer. Then the talk drifted to national affairs.

After long deliberation with the elders and with the priest, an agreement was reached to form a partisan contingent in the village, and Hailu was elected as its commander.

Not long afterward, General Abebe himself came to Menz with his strong army, who were celebrating their latest victory. With just 10,000 troops, General Abebe had defeated a 50,000 strong Italian army led by General Maltin at the Battle of Dewale. The Ethiopian army under General Abebe successfully killed thousands, captured artillery and imprisoned five Italians, including a General. General Abebe, known for his foresightedness, took measures to traverse Shewa and discuss the next phase of the struggle. He also wanted to reduce the burden of an overwrought locality by celebrating his army's victory. His presence in Menz was an extension of this strategy.

After some time, General Abebe declared that he would travel to other parts of Northern Shewa. In the meantime, Hailu met his compatriot Tewodros the Gondare. He had become a battalion commander in General Abebe's army. Hailu was very pleased with the achievement of his friend. He introduced him to his family members.

Martha was also happy to see Tewodros again. Hailu, for the first time, became suspicious that his friend and his sister were in love with each other. Tewodros asked her family her hand in marriage. The family of Martha blessed her marriage with Tewodros. After the marriage, Martha told Hailu that Tewodros had become her boyfriend while they were in General Abebe's camp in Merha Bete and Bulga. He smiled.

Martha and Tewodros spent much of their time swimming in the Adabai River. Martha showed Tewodros a nice secluded place where the two of them could enjoy themselves. She knew the place from childhood before she left for Addis Ababa. Martha took off her clothes and carried them in one hand, held high out of the water while she swam to the other side of the river. Then she sat and waited for him to come. When he was about to reach the other end, she dived into the river and swam back to the other side. Tewodros continued swimming forward, went to where Martha's clothes were, and sat on the grass. She pleaded with him to bring her clothes to her, but he kept quiet as if he has not heard her plea. She swam back to take her clothes and stood a bit far away. He ran to catch her, but she ran ahead, deep into the forest. They reappear hours later with their arms on each other's shoulders. They swam back and then returned to the village.

Tewodros informed Hailu that General Abebe had changed his plan to travel to the rest of Northern Shewa and return to Bulga.

"Why?" asked Hailu.

"He received a letter from Melake Tsehay Eyasu asking him to meet him in Bulga."

"Who is this Melake Tsehay Eyasu?"

"He is the son of the late Emperor Eyasu. He leads a partisan contingent, and the Italians were unable to win him over to their side to exploit the unfavorable relationship his father had with Emperor Haile Selassie," answered Tewodros.

General Abebe's army left to Bulga not long afterward. Martha accompanied her husband Tewodros to Bulga.

Hailu went to a nearby village for a week in an attempt to win partisans for the cause of the struggle. He was able to recruit more people. With the coming of the third anniversary of the protracted war and with the unrelenting Italian attacks, the mobilization of peasants to take arms was becoming cumbersome. With his forty followers and the blessing of his village elders and the priest, Hailu emerged as a respectable, patriotic leader.

It was emboldened with such achievements that Hailu began his journey back home. At almost halfway through the journey, he saw his brother coming towards him. Hailu wondered where Wolde was going and at the same time worried that something bad may have happened to one of the wounded commanders.

"What happened? Are the wounded in trouble?" asked Hailu, before greeting his brother. He knew that Wolde would not simply leave his village unless there was some urgent matter.

"Nothing happened to them. Our aunt sent me to inform you about new developments."

"What developments?"

"She told me that Major Mesfin and the Captain both felt you offended them. She heard them talking about you. They accused you of a breach of discipline by leaving your post to go to another village without asking for their permission. Secondly, they thought it was your duty to stand guard over their safety."

The next day, Hailu arrived in his village and went to his former commanders, pretending he did not know about their accusation. He expected them to raise the issue, but they never did.

After a while, Hailu saluted them and proceeded to leave the room; however, Major Mesfin suddenly called him back, "I want to send you on an errand," he said. He gave him a letter and told him to take it to Taitu, Meseret's and Mahlet's grandmother, in Nib Washa. Hailu complied.

Hailu took five of the newly recruited members and left for Nib Washa. He wondered whether the honeybee colonies in that village would be as enormous as he had heard. The five men went up the mountainous gorge to visit friends in villages built within two steps of the gorge. Hailu reached Nib Washa and looked back at Adabai. It was thrilling and breathtaking scenery.

He arrived at Taitu's house and saw the remains of the house burned out and a new hut built as a temporary residence for Taitu. The effects of the aerial bombardment by the Italians were evident everywhere.

"I have been informed that you were a member of the Imperial Bodyguards. Were you in Maichew?" she asked him. When he answered in the affirmative, Taitu proceeded to ask him a series of questions about her missing son.

He told her that he had neither seen nor met him in Maichew. He did however mention the fact that millions of soldiers and civilians were martyred. He added that he and his friends are still in arms to oust the Italians from Ethiopia.

She began to cry; he was at a loss for words. She, at last, asked him about the purpose of his visit.

Hailu handed her the letter from Major Mesfin Sileshi. She asked him about the Major's condition. He told her that he was fine. She called in the priest so he could read her the letter.

"My son went to Maichew, and he never returned," she said, raising the issue one more time. She raised her head and finally changed the subject. She then asked him a peculiar question, "Are you the one who has advised the peasants not to pay what is owed to the Patriarch?"

"It is not my rule. It was ruled by the partisans all over the country."

"That is not correct. I will inform this mischief to Major Mesfin. He will correct it."

"The rule only applies for the traitors to the motherland. Loyal subjects are not expropriated," added Hailu, making it clear that the rule does not apply to loyalists like hers.

"Let it be. These are trying times," she said dejectedly. Then she smiled and continued. "Do you know Meseret and Mahlet? They are my daughters. They are fighters," she referred to Meseret and Mahlet, her granddaughters, as her daughters as it is culturally appropriate to address all young relatives as one's children.

"I last met Mrs. Meseret with her husband in Merha Bete. They are doing fine."

"Good! Very good," said Taitu satisfied that her granddaughters were well and alive.

"I have planned to return to my village early next morning. I am happy to comply with the wishes of my Lady," Hailu said.

She called in her maidservant and told her something surreptitiously. The servant disappeared for a moment, and then returned with a bundle of homemade cotton blankets. Taitu gave the blankets to Hailu, instructing him to give it to Major Mesfin and his friends and then added, "Tell him that I will come one of these days and visit him."

Hailu bowed his head in salute and then left.

He went to the Saint Mary church in the Jer and Nib Washa village to make a short prayer and start his travels homeward. Kahn Yohannes could be heard preaching. He stood for a while and listened to the sermon.

"A story is told how Jesus arrived with his mother in Ethiopia via Egypt before his baptism in the River Jordan. The Book of the Archangel Raguel by Saint John, tells a story about Jesus' attendance at the synagogue in Axum along with his mother, Joseph and Salome. Zion in the Ark of the Covenant blessed him. God's will was proclaimed as a cloud that arose from the Ark of the Covenant. During their return journey, the cloud carried Mary, Jesus, Joseph and Salome back to Jerusalem. God's will was proclaimed through the dove, over the river of Jordan. During their flight back home, carried by the cloud of the Ark of the Covenant, Jesus told his mother that Ethiopians would glorify her to the end of the world. Ethiopia is a blessed country as the dwelling place of the Ark of the Covenant and the land where Saint Mary glorified to the end of time. The Italians could not defeat and colonize Ethiopia."

Hailu felt happy. He made the sign of the cross starting from his face and touching the two sides of his chest and journeyed down the Adabai Gorge to his home village.

2

Major Mesfin, Lieutenant Mekuria and Mrs. Konjit, General Abebe's wife had recuperated. They had regained their strength and got ready to return to Bulga where the army under General Abebe was currently stationed.

They discovered that while they were recuperating, Hailu had grown strong with forty followers and he was now a force to be reckoned with. At first, the Major and the Lieutenant hoped that his newly found strength would be an addition to their forces serving under General Abebe. They mentioned to him to take his followers along with him when they return to Bulga. Hailu kept quiet.

On the day, the Major and the Lieutenant left to Bulga. Hailu was not there to bid them farewell. They left for General Abebe with all the honors and logistics that befitted their position.

No one knows up to this day the arrangements between General Abebe and Hailu. People were suspicious that he might have been doing everything as ordered by General Abebe to curry favor with the Chief Commander. He took Mrs. Konjit in person to General Abebe and then returned to his village with encouraging words from the General.

Not long afterward Hailu left for Afkera with his forty soldiers. Afkera is a valley encircled by chains of mountains, which made it a natural fortification suitable as headquarters for a guerrilla movement. Hailu and his men were discussing the suitability of the place to conduct prolonged warfare. They saw Kefelew coming towards them.

Hailu had met Kefelew in Merha Bete when he came along with Beshah and Tesema to General Abebe's camp.

"I heard that when you were returning from Merha Bete you were encircled in a cave but heroically escaped," Hailu commented after they exchanged greetings.

"Yes, but I lost my wife, Asegedech."

"Did she die?" asked Hailu, aware of the Italian rule of killing every patriot after his or her capture.

"No, she was taken prisoner; she has denied that she is a patriot and is pretending to be someone else and not my wife," he said and added, "I will never rest until she is rescued."

Hailu had heard the story of his previous attempt to free her, which ended in an accidental encounter with Ephraim, a local chieftain that changed his allegiance to the Italian occupiers. Kefelew had prepared a plan to rescue Asegedech by attacking the Italian camp at Molale. At the same time, the traitor Ephraim promised the Italian commander at the Molale camp to go with his men and capture Gizachew Haile and his soldiers without the assistance of the Italians and started to move down the valley where Gizachew Haile has set up camp. At the same time, Kefelew with his soldiers was moving up the hill to Molale to rescue his wife. Kefelew observed Ephraim and his soldiers' movement and became suspicious. He ordered his soldiers to take cover and sent spies to bring information. Ephraim hurried to where Gizachew was to launch a surprise attack. Kefelew readied his soldiers for an ambush. Kefelew's soldiers apprehended and imprisoned Ephraim and his soldiers without firing a shot.

Kefelew brought the chief before Gizachew Haile, who confined him to a house arrest.

"I know you will succeed in your endeavor. We would like to help you any way we could;" said Hailu.

"Hailu, I have a favor to ask. One of my machineguns is not working. As a member of the Imperial Bodyguards, you must be familiar with this type of machinegun. Could you try to repair it?"

Hailu brought an ox skin hide and put it on the ground. Then put the machinegun on it and disassembled it. He greased it and put it back together again after finding no serious defect. "It seems fine, it should work," said Hailu.

"Please test it," demanded Kefelew.

Hailu loaded it and successfully fired a few rounds. Kefelew was happy.

Around glasses of Ethiopian beer, they exchanged ideas on different topics. Kefelew told Hailu how he was a student in Emperor Menelik's school in Addis Ababa, and how he interrupted his education in the 4th grade to come to the rural areas to help his father in matters of land litigation in the courts. He also told him that General Kebede gave him the machinegun.

Hailu also told him about his life in Addis Ababa.

"Why don't we work together?" Kefelew suggested. "If we merge our forces we could facilitate the liberation of our country effectively."

"I would love to but..." Hailu mused.

This was unthinkable before General Kebede submitted to the Italians. Currently with small towns occupied by the Italians, a mixed strategy, which gave equal emphasis to both conventional and guerrilla warfare, was been adopted. In the conventional structure, soldiers belonged to their battalions and their allegiance was to the Ethiopian army and the Emperor, not to field commanders. With the newly formed guerrilla units here in Menz, a new form of coordination had replaced the traditional one. Each guerrilla unit had become virtually autonomous, working individually to strengthen its respective unit. The new guerrilla units depended for sustenance on their tribes and localities. Gizachew, who had been prominent during the conventional warfare, had begun to adopt guerrilla tactics.

"What reasons do you have? You may state them?" Kefelew insisted.

"Your ways of leadership are different from what we currently exercise as ordered by General Abebe. You force the peasants to slaughter their sheep and oxen for you," said Hailu.

"How could we continue the struggle without nourishment?"

"If we offend the peasants, they will feel alienated, and some of them will even defect to the Italians. That would spell big trouble for us. It is a blessing to enter a home where a fire is made even if there is no food," said Hailu, putting his ideas in the context of an ancient proverb. He was explaining the need to keep the population in the non-Italian-occupied territories from leaving to Italian-occupied towns.

"That is very true. However, do you have a better alternative?"

"We should not expropriate the peasant's property. Some ex-landlords have their allegiances to the Italians in the cities where they live. We could expropriate their properties and land."

Kefelew agreed.

"My case may be cited," Hailu continued. "My ancestor's lands were illegally transferred to the archbishop and since the outbreak of war, he has left to Egypt. We expropriated his property and land. We used the income to buy bullets and rifles necessary to fight this war."

"This could be done," said Kefelew.

Hailu felt he had Kefelew's consent. However, he also felt that he might have a difficult time selling his idea to others, convincing them to change their habitual practices of expropriation. Personal interests, regional realities, and national responsibilities were colliding in this complicated environment. After this, Kefelew and Hailu agreed in principle to work together.

Months passed since Kefelew left to go to Imweta. One day Hailu saw armed people passing over the hill above his village. "Gizachew and Kefelew are leading their partisans to Keya Gabriel to oust or capture the callous Italian appointed Ethiopian administrator."

"Let's go then and join them. We shouldn't wait until we are asked to participate."

"Yes, you're right," agreed Hailu's soldiers.

Hailu mobilized his men and joined Gizachew and Kefelew.

When the moon disappeared and darkness lay over the land, Gizachew Haile, as chief commander, ordered the partisans to attack.

"Don't forget to send all cattle and sheep to the Adabai river bed."

"Why is that?" Hailu asked Kefelew.

"Chief Isayas, the traitor, has expropriated the cattle and grain of loyal citizens so we must avenge his treachery. Secondly, we have to make the people in the village declare their loyalty and willingness to the Imperial Government so that they will pay the necessary taxes and duties."

Hailu was impressed.

The partisans moved in a big semi-circle firing and throwing hand grenades. Others were driving the cattle toward the river. Fire, cries and dust filled the night. Hailu reached Chief Isayas's house.

"Where is the traitor?" Hailu heard Gizachew's voice.

"He heard the shootings and was informed about your coming, he ordered his horse to be ready, and he rode off to the Italian camp.

"How many people have followed him?"

"He went alone."

"Give up your rifles and you will remain prisoners," Gizachew addressed the soldiers of Chief Isayas.

Hailu admired Gizachew, the brave son of Menz. A general assembly, called on the next day, agreed on the treatment of the prisoners and the people of Keya Gabriel. Gizachew ordered the prisoners to appear. Hailu waited to see how Gizachew would handle the situation.

"You have fought against us and betrayed your religion and country by being instruments of the enemy," Gizachew addressed the prisoners. He told them the history of the country, the nature of the present war and their responsibility as Ethiopians. Hailu read from the faces of the prisoners their deep emotions. Gizachew concluded, "Those of you who want to join the struggle is welcome and your rifles will be returned to you. Those of you who do not want to join us can leave to your village. Your rifles are needed for the struggle and are therefore expropriated."

Hailu was deeply impressed with Gizachew's performance.

The people of Keya Gabriel paid their dues and declared their loyalty to the Imperial Ethiopian Government.

After a week, Gizachew left to Imweta and Kefelew stayed behind as Hailu's guest.

Two days after Gizachew returned to Imweta, Kefelew mentioned to Hailu the need to formalize their previous understanding to work together.

"I think now is the right time," agreed Hailu.

A general meeting of the partisans under Kefelew, Hailu, and the other commander's chose Kefelew as the main commander and Hailu as vice-commander. Section commanders bestowed with governorship of specified areas were satisfied with the arrangement.

This division of territories between partisan leaders was a new development in the resistance war. This led to clashes amongst partisan leaders and its effect continued to affect the struggle for the coming two years.

"Before concluding the agreement I think we should in reverence to our customs of displaying our allegiance to one another, get a jar of beer and select buds of plants that represent each of the Holy Saints. We will prepare feasts in their honor and in honor of our allegiance to each other," Kefelew said.

Hailu went out and brought five sticks with leaves on them. Each stick representing the tabots of the archangels Michael, Gabriel, Raguel, Saint Tekle Haimanot, and Saint Mary were ready for a lottery draw. The lottery drawing from the five sticks would be the tabot to commemorate their alliance.

"Who is to draw the lottery?" asked Hailu.

"It is better to ask a child to do so. Children are God's favorites," said Tekle.

A small boy found nearby drew the lottery. The boy drew one of the sticks and gave it to Kefelew. The stick with only one leaf, assigned to Archangel Gabriel, was drawn.

"Bring the jar of beer," Kefelew said. The priest blessed the jar and gave it to Kefelew. He drank from it and passed it to the person sitting next to him, and the jar passed around the table until everyone had a sip. Thereafter, the priest presented the blessed bread, said a prayer, and then passed it around the table. They all ate. This was the symbol of the flesh and blood of the Redeemer, Jesus Christ. With this act of goodwill and congruity, they made a vow to remain loyal to one another.

The Kahn of the church of the archangel Gabriel rose up and gave his blessing. He lectured them on their responsibility to God and their country.

3

It was on the morrow Wolde reminded Hailu that it had been three years since the Italian fascists invaded Ethiopia. The information was meant to remind Hailu about the forecast by the monks that Italy would remain in Ethiopia for three years and then will be defeated when God showed his mercy for his chosen people.

Hailu seemed not to capture the reason why Wolde raised the issue. "It seemed ages, much more than three years ago," he answered.

"This is the year the monks predicted the mercy of God and Ethiopia ousting the Italians."

Hailu remembered and smiled. It is three years since the forecast.

It was not long after this conversation that information came that the Italian commander in Molale garrison has been assassinated.

"I don't think they are false rumors," Wolde replied.

"Why don't you send somebody and verify it?" Hailu asked.

"I will do that. Look Kefelew is coming towards us. Why don't you go and meet him."

"Sure," said Hailu and went towards Kefelew.

"Hailu, have you heard that the Emperor has come back with French forces over the Ogaden," Kefelew said.

"Tesema Irgete also said the same thing to the people of Yifat ten days after the Emperor left to Europe," Hailu facetiously remarked.

"But this time it may be true."

"I wish it was. But it may be false and may damage the morale of the peasants if false hopes are circulated among them."

"You are correct," said Kefelew and looked at the setting sun. Hailu followed his eye.

The sky silhouetted by the setting sun turned red. Both Hailu and Kefelew, infused with a new sense of purpose, felt renewed determination. Maybe it was the result of the recent victories over the Italians that boosted their morale, or perhaps it was the assembly of allegiance a few days ago that ultimately strengthened the bonds between the partisans. But for whatever reason, Kefelew, Hailu and their constituents' at large felt victory was within reach. The trying times they had endured, the Battle at Maichew, the perfidious traitors, the exodus of the Emperor all seemed for a larger purpose destined by God.

"I am confident we will win this war," Kefelew declared. "Hailu, by the way, do you know people from this region who are serving the Italians at Sasit camp?"

"There are many. Some went there to earn their bread. Their hearts are with us though."

"I need people just like that."

"Why do you need them? Is it to plant spies over there? We already have people serving in such positions."

"More than that," Kefelew replied.

"Then for what purpose do you need them?" Hailu insisted.

"You know that my wife, Asegedech, is still a prisoner of the Italians. She has been transferred to Sasit camp; I need all the help I can find to get my wife back," Kefelew explained. "Why don't you contact those villagers working for the Italians? They might be able to help me rescue my wife"

"I will try," said Hailu.

"What you are doing is not as a personal favor."

"I understand it is not a personal favor. When we try to free our compatriots from the enemy we are performing our sacred patriotic duty."

A plan was formulated to free Kefelew's wife. Ethiopians working with the Italians sympathetic to the partisans came forward. At night, the partisans approached the camp and opened fire upon the Italians at Sasit camp. Two Ethiopian defectors handed over Kefelew's wife to the partisans. The partisans retreated with Kefelew's wife safely.

Kefelew, as chief commander, spent his time on administrative issues. Hailu, using Kefelew's machinegun, became responsible for conducting military operations. Kefelew and Hailu had successfully fought many battles together. Gizachew Haile was still the chief coordinator of the partisan struggle in Menz, Yifat, and Tegulet.

One day, Hailu came across a meeting headed by Gizachew Haile. Hailu observed one of the front guards handing a letter to Gizachew. Gizachew's face darkened in anger as he read the letter handed to him. Hailu questioned a friend about the letter that caused Gizachew to be angry. The friend informed him that the letter was captured from the servant of the traitor chief from Menz, under house arrest. It was addressed to the Italian commander in Molale.

"How did the front guard find the letter?" asked Hailu.

"The servant of the chief was caught when he tried to pass it over to the Italians. He was captured and searched."

Hailu decided not to inquire any further.

Not long afterward, a general meeting of all the partisans assembled. Gizachew interrogated the chief who appeared in handcuffs. Gizachew presented the letter and asked the chief about it.

"Yes, it is a letter written by me," answered the chief in defiance. The chief had been under house arrest for some time.

"You belittled our favors, which were granted to you because of our past friendship."

"I don't need advice from people of your type," the chief insolently replied.

"Why don't you work with us hand-in-hand for the motherland rather than serving our enemies?" Gizachew persisted.

"I don't want to ally with bandits of your type. Long live the enlightened Italian Regime," the chief defiantly said.

Gizachew lost his temper. He took his machinegun from his aid, pointed it directly at the chief, and asked, "What did you say?"

"I said what I said," the chief answered.

Gizachew fired, directly, at the chief, killing him instantly.

A silence ensued.

"Brothers," said Gizachew, "from now on, we have to return their mischief with mischief; an eye for an eye. Every one of us is equal as far as blood is concerned. Kings may favor some of us and appoint us as chiefs, but that does not mean that people of this region are composed of different stocks. Chiefs who betray us in favor of the Italians will be treated as any other traitor."

"Correct!" cheered the partisans, still bristling over the traitor's insolent remarks. Gizachew, who usually treated the captured traitors with respect and dignity, could not bear the site of anyone, let alone an Ethiopian, showing reverence for the Italian Empire.

[141]

Not long afterward, Kefelew ordered an offensive against a traitor named Gebre. Kefelew and Hailu mobilized their forces and marched to Gebre's hideout. Gebre informed about the partisans' incursion, fled to the Italian resident's officer in Yifat for protection. The partisans appropriated Gebre's property and they took his daughter.

Months passed without a word from Gebre. Then one day Hailu, returning from camp, saw Gebre sitting beside Kefelew.

"How did Gebre come here?" Hailu asked bewildered at the unexpected scene.

"Well, he heard that Kefelew had taken his daughter as his mistress, and so he believes that Kefelew is his son-in-law," responded one of the soldiers with him.

"Please take some more tej (wine made from honey); it will be good for you," Hailu heard Kefelew saying to Gebre.

Hailu left to a nearby village for inspection duties. While Hailu was making his journey back to the camp, a partisan informed him about Gebre's assassination by an unknown individual. Hailu hurried to Kefelew and asked him what happened.

"Gebre has been assassinated," Kefelew replied. "Look at this paper." Kefelew handed the letter to Hailu.

Hailu read the letter. It was a letter written from the Italian resident officer in Yifat to the resident officer in Molale. The letter listed the many contributions Gebre made to the Italian cause and asked the Molale resident officer to give Gebre support. Hailu looked at Kefelew and asked, "How did you obtain this letter?"

"The wine and alcoholic drinks loosened his tongue, and he told me and handed me this letter," said Kefelew handing the letter to Hailu. "Then I told him to go to the grain silo to pick up the grain that I have ordered my men to provide him with. When he left, I sent soldiers behind him."

This was a great time for Hailu. His new friends were not only faithful to the struggle but also ruthless in their dealings with traitors, making potential traitors think twice before confronting them. They began planning retributions on communities who changed allegiance from the liberators to Italians. The first target was Jamma district in Yifat.

Gizachew Haile, Teshome Shenkute, Kefelew and Hailu as one of the battalion commanders, launched an offensive against traitors.

The journey to Jamma began.

If Jamma is liberated the patriots will bring a territory rich in resources under their control and will be able to open up a trade route to Afar and Eastern Ethiopia.

The partisans marched throughout the night. At dawn, they finally reached the border of Jamma.

The partisans had information about the guards of the Italian garrison found deep in Jamma. The guards were locally recruited bandas. The forward guards were soldiers belonging to the chief of the city, who betrayed the Ethiopians earlier.

The partisans moved up, forming a wide circle around the escarpment. They finally reached the top of the escarpment but wondered how they were able to come so far without any hindrances from the bandas. Undeterred, the partisans subsequently opened fire, targeting the bandas. They then marched further into Jamma, pilfering the villagers' cattle. The Italians in the garrison opened artillery fire against the partisans but were too afraid to move out from their camps.

A few moments after the attack, the Italians retreated; a local chieftain emerged along with many of his equestrians.

"Identify yourself," Kefelew said when the chieftain reached the near distance.

"I am a partisan from this region. I came to assist you," the chieftain replied.

Kefelew ordered his soldiers to disarm the chieftain and his followers.

"I am a partisan working under General Abebe Aregai. My name is Captain Tegegne Busera."

"That will be verified later on. For the present you are under arrest," said Kefelew and dismissed him.

During the night, the people of Jamma came to plead with the partisans for the return of their cattle. The partisans asked them why they had stopped paying the taxes due to the Ethiopian government. The villagers did not have a credible excuse for their actions. Instead, they pledged to pay the arrears and subsequent taxes. The partisans decided that the local population has to pay taxes in kind, mostly in bullets and bushels of grain. The cattle were returned to the owners after settling the taxes imposed.

Then a council gathered and heard Tegegne Busera's case. Tegegne appealed before the council to have his machinegun returned and, because he was a patriot, to be cleared of any charges of treason. Kefelew, however, insisted that Tegegne only pretended to be a patriot after he saw the defeat of the Italians and that he had killed his soldier three years ago, and deserves the death sentence.

Gizachew Haile felt Kefelew's accusations against Tegegne inappropriate and aimed to expropriate his machinegun. Gizachew consulted with the Council members and they referred the case to General Abebe. They decided also that Tegegne Busera be handed over to Teshome Shenkute, and ordered him remain with Teshome until General Abebe gave a final decision. In the meantime, Tegegne's machinegun was appropriated and given to Kefelew.

After the war council, Kefelew met with Hailu and said to him, "Hailu, you should return my machinegun as you can now use Tegegne's machinegun for your division."

Hailu agreed.

Thus, Kefelew and Hailu became better armed with an extra machinegun. They moved to the lowlands, while Teshome Shenkute along with Tegegne Busera, left for Merha Bete to appear before General Abebe Aregai.

On the way back to Merha Bete, Teshome Shenkute was attacked by the Italians from the ground and the air with chemicals. The Italians sprayed mustard gas on the soldiers and the area at large. Teshome Shenkute ordered his army and the population with their cattle to take shelter in a large cave found in the area. The Italian artilleries bombed the cave through its entrance with canisters filled with mustard and phosgene gas. Thousands perished through suffocation by mustard and phosgene gas. Teshome Shenkute and few others survived the chemical attack and escaped from the cave.

Within a week, the news reached to Kefelew and Hailu.

"What about Tegegne Busera, who was with Teshome?" Hailu asked.

"He was one of the survivors from the cave. He went to General Abebe Aregai with Teshome Shenkute."

The information was confirmed when General Abebe wrote a letter to Kefelew demanding the restoration of Tegegne's machinegun. Kefelew was offended.

"I think we have to abide by General Abebe's decision and return the machinegun to Tegegne Busera;" Hailu suggested when Kefelew asked him for advice.

"No. We will write a letter demanding that the war council consider the case. We will buy time through such means."

Hailu remembered Kefelew's experience with litigation at court. Kefelew had told him when they met in Afkera how he was assisting his father in his litigation over land in the courts before the Italians invaded Ethiopia.

"We will not return the machinegun at any cost," Kefelew concluded.

4

At the end of the month, Hailu was conducting routine inspections of military units in the border areas of Menz and Merha Bete a battle commenced in a nearby place. He hurried with his men to where the fighting was raging. He discovered that his former bodyguard commanders, Major Mesfin Sileshi and Captain Mekuria's battalions were blocking an Italian rush forward down the valley to attack the main Command Post. Hailu and his men maneuvered and stationed themselves behind the enemy line.

The fighting was intense. Hailu's machinegun fire from behind overwhelmed the Italians. A unit assigned to counter Hailu's unit brought to a halt his machinegun attack. Hailu passed over the machinegun to his brother Wolde and started to use his rifle. Wolde saw an Italian climbing to where they were and decided to change position. He rose and ran while firing his machinegun. Hailu quickly followed his brother. Captain Mengesha gave them cover with machinegun fire. The courageous maneuvers by Hailu and his men forced the Italians to retreat.

Captain Mengesha met Hailu and patted him on the shoulder said, "How are you Hailu?"

Hailu stood at attention and saluted, "How do you do sir?" he replied.

"We are proud of you," said his former commander. He did not mention their last encounter when wounded and convalescing at Hailu's place. Hailu said farewell and returned to his home.

When Hailu reached his village, he found Kefelew angry and agitated.

"General Abebe has sent another letter ordering the restoration of Tegegne's machinegun," said Kefelew after exchanging greetings.

"What does the letter specifically state?"

"He is ordering me to appear before him and answer the charges made against me,"

"What did you decide?"

"I will not go and handover myself over to him."

"General Abebe may take this as an insult," Hailu mentioned

No one had ever dared to refuse General Abebe's orders; he was a powerful leader, much loved by his people and feared by the Italians.

Weeks passed without a word from General Abebe. Then in June of 1938, information reached Kefelew that General Abebe was coming to Menz. Hailu feared that General Abebe was coming to punish them for their insubordination over the return of Tegegne Busera's machinegun.

The partisans around the region began to write letters to Kefelew pleading with him to solve his problem with General Abebe.

Later, it was discovered that General Abebe not only wanted Kefelew to answer the charges brought about by Tegegne Busera, but also required all commanders in Yifat, Menz and Tegulet to respond about their overall practice to divide the region into fiefs and collect government taxes for their own battalion's use. General Abebe considered this an act of banditry.

Hailu felt guilty for agreeing and adopting illegal practices. He knew he was in a very precarious situation.

Part Six: The Comrade in Arms
Meseret / Hailu

1

It has been a year since Beshah's army left Menz and Tegulet and made its Headquarters in Bulga and Merha Bete. Meseret was impressed with the natural beauty of Bulga and its surroundings. The land was very beautiful with lush green plants, trees, and mountains. She cut a twig from a bush they locally called 'kese' smelled it, and said to herself, "A plant that grows in my birthplace is also found here!" Her brightened face was accentuated by its contrast with her hand-woven traditional white cotton dress and a scarf, bordered with red, which gently blew in the wind. Her husband, Samuel, seeing her in this relaxed, light-hearted mood, approached her quietly. He stood behind her for a moment, unnoticed, then took the rifle from his shoulder and cautiously put the leather strip over her shoulder and left the rifle dangling on her waist. He burst out laughing.

"What are you doing?" she asked.

"Just stand as before. I want to see you carrying a rifle."

"Haven't you ever seen me with a rifle?"

"Not amidst green leaves and colorful flowers.''

She smiled. "You look very beautiful in dresses. Those trousers and that coat do not befit such an elegant lady," he said. "By the way, what made you so happy to laugh and smile alone?" he added, making it clear from his tone that he liked her current disposition.

"The landscape is beautiful, isn't it?"

"Beauty is in the eye of the beholder," he said, remembering how Meseret was gloomy after the Italians had taken Mahlet as a prisoner.

"Where do we go next?" she asked him in a tactful attempt to change the topic of discussion.

"We will stay in Bulga. The European educated elites with General Abebe's army have studied and presented strategies for conducting the war to oust the Italians from the towns and the cities. Meetings will be held throughout the month so I think we will have to stay in beautiful Bulga."

"I heard that European educated elites convert to Catholicism. I do not consider any good idea will come out of people who change their father's religion."

He kept quiet

"Is it true that these intellectuals eat pork?" she persisted.

"They have learned the wisdom of the white man, but they are still Orthodox Christians. They do not eat pork. The white man you saw with General Abebe is a Russian, and he is an Orthodox Christian. Some Orthodox Christians like the Russians eat pork. British nationals led by Mrs. Sylvia Pankhurst assist the Emperor in England. Her organization has mobilized supporters from all over the world. She loves Ethiopia, and she has struggled for Ethiopia."

The British woman impressed Meseret. "She is a blessed woman. I will pray for her always. I will even commemorate Saint Michael of November in her name," Meseret declared.

He smiled and kept quiet.

"By the way, what was the idea the foreign-educated elites proposed to General Abebe?" Meseret asked.

"You know a hive without the queen bee cannot survive. We are also like worker bees without a leader. We need a leader."

"We have our Emperor, don't we? Didn't you tell me that he has gone abroad, but he will return and has ordered us to fight in his name?"

"Anyway queen bee outside her hive is as good as dead," Samuel purported. She remained silent. Samuel continued, "General Abebe is with Melake Tsehay Eyasu at this moment. He will most likely be appointed as Commander-in-chief."

"Who is Melake Tsehay Eyasu?"

"He is the grandson of Emperor Menelik ll. He is the son of Lij Eyasu. The Italians tried to bribe him to join them, but he refused. He is a well-known patriot leader. His father was a great patriot as well. He worked to push out the Italians, French, and British, all conquerors of the blessed lands of Africa. His grandfather Lij Eyasu failed, but the ideas he promoted were which he inherited from Menelik the II and General Gobena."

The following days were frantic. The former Imperial Bodyguard Units whose numbers were significant, serving under General Abebe army, were brought together to show impressive military parades.

The assignment of Melake Tsehay Eyasu as Commander-in-chief caused division and animosity within the Ethiopian armies. General Haile Mariam Mammo, who stationed his army in Adama and the surrounding areas, defiantly declared that the appointment of Melake Tsehay as Commander-in-chief whiles the Emperor was still alive conducting a diplomatic struggle in Europe, was an ill-found measure.

In the ensuing days, a big ceremony was held in commemoration of Melake Tsehay Eyasu's appointment as Commander-in-chief of the Ethiopian Army.

It was a lively ceremony. The partisans and peasants came out to celebrate this moment, and even Meseret and Samuel forgot the case of General Haile Mariam Mammo and the whole opposition.

After fifteen days, General Abebe endowed the Military titles upon several of his followers. He even gave governorship titles to some of them.

General Abebe bestowed the title of the governorship of a province upon Haile Mariam Mammo. Haile Mariam Mammo rejected the appointment and declared that his contingents have severed their relations with the General Abebe-led Army.

Samuel shared his fear to Meseret in these trying days. "I do not know what is to be done? I am afraid that war will break out amongst us."

"Well, General Haile Mariam is not in a region nearby, and secondly there will not be victors if ever the two forces engage, therefore it is unfounded to fear military encounters between Generals Abebe and Haile Mariam," she observed.

Samuel smiled, "You are either a witch or an angel!"

"An angel!" she replied.

After the appointment of Melake Tsehay Eyasu as chief commander, Meseret spent her time observing the organization and strength of General Abebe's army.

Meseret found General Abebe's camp enlightened and disciplined. Even though most of the partisans were Oromos and Amharas, there was a wide representation of all ethnic groups. There were Eritreans, who defected from the Italians. The daughter of the Tigrai Governor Ras Seyoum Mengesha, Mrs. Kebedetch Seyoum was a famous partisan leader there. There were Russian and British visitors who came to the camp from time to time to provide support. General Abebe had a good relationship with all of the Generals and mobile guerrilla leaders in Gojjam, Gondar, Tigrai, Wollo, Harar, Bale, and Wollega. His secret service extended to Djibouti and Sudan. He was even able to communicate with the Emperor through the British-Ethiopian support group of Sylvia Pankhurst.

On the next day, the spymaster in Addis Ababa, Tekle came to General Abebe camp. Meseret insisted that he dine with them. He was familiar with her interests and told her about the patriots' struggle in the other parts of Ethiopia.

He told her about the renowned patriots that commanded hundreds of soldiers such as Abay Kahsay in Tigrai, Umer Semeter in Ogaden, and Geresu Duki in west Addis Ababa and Jimma. In Begemider, General Woubeneh Tesema, like General Abebe, controlled the rural areas and was effectively pinning the Italians within the towns. He told her that in Wag, General Hailu Kebede was leading the struggle. He told her that the Gondaries were fighting tooth and nail throughout Begemider and in the frontier lands in the south.

Meseret was impressed with the story he told her about the battle fought to liberate Addis Ababa three years earlier, two months after the Italians occupied the capital. It was a very heroic feat, even if unsuccessful. The Ethiopian Orthodox Bishop His Holiness Pope Petros taken prisoner had died a hero's death in the hands of the Fascists; he condemned the fascist act and instructed the Ethiopians to continue the struggle.

The most important news Tekle brought from Addis Ababa was that the British and French had declared war on Germany on September 3, 1939, and that the German-Italian-Japanese alliance on September 27, 1939, could lead the USA to abandon her neutrality to keep her interest in the Far East.

The Italian all-out offensive that took place in Northern Shewa before the onslaught of the British stopped the war between Haile Mariam's and General Abebe's forces.

Meseret and Samuel were home with their friends when a peasant came and announced that the Commander in Chief Melake Tsehay Eyasu, had died from cholera.

The condemnation of Italy by the League of Nations and Italy's withdrawal from the League of Nations strengthened the position of Emperor Haile Selassie among the patriots. No other Commander-in-chief was ever appointed thereafter. The Ethiopian armies everywhere were engaged in fierce defensive battles against the Italians.

2

A small military contingent that included Meseret and Samuel was assigned to the task of secretly burying the deceased Commander-in-chief, since the Italian offensive had already started. The current offensive of the fascist Italians was extensive, engaging most of the Ethiopian patriots and the formidable army of General Abebe. Intensive aerial artillery bombardment with mustard gas and flamethrowers was extensively used. The Italians were trying to force an armistice on the Ethiopian army and if possible, destroy it before they faced the British and French forces.

The chemical bombardment from artillery and airplane depended on napalm, a gelatinous substance that combined naphthelmic and palmitc acids and gasoline. This was a very effective and brutal deterrent on an army, which had been sprayed with this liquid from the air and then ignited with flamethrowers. General Abebe's army dispersed in the vast surrounding areas and took shade under stones and trees while encircling the enemy from every direction. The army avoided the poisonous bombardment by positioning itself against the direction of the wind in addition to dispersing in vast areas of the countryside.

The ensuing battle raged on violently for three days, with both sides suffering heavy casualties. Airplane bombardment had stopped one day earlier, which the Ethiopian army understood to be due to the enemy's depleted arsenal.

The Italians seemed reinvigorated; they were determined to win this battle after a series of defeats. Eventually, the Ethiopian Army found itself encircled by the Italians. After burying the late Commander-in-chief, Samuel's contingent joined the battlefront. Meseret found the battle with the Italians a test of courage. This somehow gave her more energy and transformed the imminent danger into an admirable task of dying with honor.

She heard a war cry coming from her left. She assumed that the Italians had broken the resistance line. She turned around to find out that the partisan contingents of Ayele Haile and Desta Shewa Erkabech were in fact the ones who had broken the Italian encirclement.

The Ethiopian army ordered to retreat to Menz, followed the Adabai River Gorge in a defensive retreat. Two battalions from the surrounding area counter encircled the Italians on the south and east, which led the Italian commander to halt its army from following the retreating Ethiopian army into the Adabai River Gorge.

Meseret tried to evaluate the situation, and she said to her husband, "Samuel, don't you think that fate is guiding us back to our birthplace for a good reason?"

"Maybe" he said. She did not continue the discussion.

Meseret suddenly grabbed her stomach in pain.

"What happened?" asked Samuel remembering that Meseret had told him two months earlier that she was pregnant. There was also a cholera epidemic that killed Melake Tsehay.

"I am ok. It was just an ache."

Meseret was ill for some time, but she did not tell anyone. She did not want to be a burden on the soldiers, who were already tired and weak from battle. These were trying times.

The army led by General Abebe trekked the bed of the Adabai River for three days with meager rations. Some contingents left for the unenviable task of searching for food in the nearby villages, but they were unsuccessful.

Only one search team returned with sacks of beans in the morning to distribute among the hungry partisans. Each partisan received a handful of beans. Meseret took her share and the share of her uncle Beshah, who was praying.

Beshah finished his meditation then sat up straight and opened his eyes. He looked at his surroundings with a tranquil spirit.

"Good morning Meseret," he said when he saw her standing in front of him.

"Good morning Uncle. I have brought your share of beans."

"What share?"

"Some beans for your breakfast."

He accepted the handful of beans. Three days had passed since he last ate, and that was only a raw banana. After the first two days without food, he felt weak, and the pangs of hunger had become unbearably painful.

Suddenly, the voice of an agitated priest reverberated throughout the camp.

"This Hyena type of person has eaten all my beans," the priest said, looking at Abate.

"Well, I thought you put them aside not interested to eat them. I was hungry, so I ate them," Abate said, ashamed of his action.

"I was praying and planned to eat them after prayer." After a few short moments, the priest calmed down. "Anyway, I am not angry with you. I was just joking. Beans less than half a handful are not that important," said the priest.

Meseret went to the priest and without being seen, put some beans over his scarf and left.

The priest after finishing reading his bible rose pulling up his long scarf (shema). He observed the beans that fell from his shema. He rapaciously picked them up, eating each one he found before he picked up the other. "I thought that hyena-natured person ate all my beans!" After eating each remaining bean as if it were his last meal, he picked up his rifle and jokingly pointed it at Abate. "I would have finished you, hyena, had you eaten all of my beans."

The partisan contingents began their march, leaving the Adabai River. When they moved up to the promontory, Meseret looked down and saw the milky water of the Adabai River that would turn brown in a few months after the ferocious winter rains wash away all the mud from the mountains and carry it into the river.

The Shewa army led by General Abebe extricated itself from a perilous encirclement and then attacked the Italian with renewed strength and forced them to retreat and shelter themselves in the towns. In those weeks, General Abebe received letters from his brothers, generals in Gojjam, Jimma, Harar, Tigray, Wollo, Kaffa and many more enumerating how they had frustrated the Italians last attempt to defeat them. In all the letters, there was something referring to the mercy of God. It mentions that the European war had started and expressed their hope that God will avenge the crimes against the dwelling place of the Ark of the Covenant and its chosen people. It must have been an extension of Emperor Haile Selassie's speech in Geneva three years ago. At the League of Nations, the Emperor emphasized that the sacrificing of Ethiopia for a momentary peace, will lead the Europeans to face a formidable enemy.

The army moved to the plains. When they reached the top of the mountain, Meseret threw herself on the plain, and too exhausted to set up a proper tent, she quickly fell asleep. She did not know how long she slept for, but she was tormented with horrible dreams of war, hunger, and misery. In one of her dreams, she was taken as a prisoner and met Mahlet. In the dream, she sat behind Mahlet who turns around and looks at her. They do not say a word to each other. An Italian soldier suddenly approaches Meseret and orders her to stand, but she simply ignores him. The soldier violently pulls her up by her hair.

She then awoke and saw the smiling face of her husband Samuel.

"Eat this bread," he said to her.

"Where did you get it?"

"The people of the region brought us food while you were asleep. Guess who was among them?"

"How would I know?"

"They are Kefelew and Hailu," he said reminding her about the case of Tegegne Busera's machinegun.

"How did General Abebe react?" she asked, remembering the letter Kefelew and General

Abebe exchanged and Kefelew's refusal to appear before General Abebe, who summoned him to respond to charges why he had not returned Tegegne Busera's machinegun as ordered.

Not long afterward, Hailu and another man came to visit Samuel and Meseret. The person who came with Hailu was Tadesse, the husband of Meseret's niece, Fana.

Meseret was surprised to see Hailu without Tegegne Busera's machinegun because she had heard that he carried it wherever he went. "Where is the machinegun of Tegegne Busera?" asked Meseret, seeing Hailu with only a rifle dangling from his shoulder.

"They might have thought it was more appropriate not to bring it to avoid offending Tegegne Busera and General Abebe," Samuel answered.

"Yes. That must be," said Meseret and went forward to meet Tadesse.

"Is Fana fine? Are you ok?" asked Meseret intentionally using the male pronoun to refer to her niece. Her grandmother bore many children, but many of them died during childhood. The witch doctors advised her grandmother that the bad spirits, who were responsible for the deaths of her children, could be fooled if her male children were clothed and addressed as female and the female children were clothed and addressed as male. Therefore, the grandmother established this norm among her family, a norm Meseret still honored.

Meseret introduced Samuel and Tadesse to each other.

They all took their seats and began to talk. It was not long before Samuel raised the affair of the machinegun, a case that has been the source of some tension between General Abebe and Kefelew.

"Well... we didn't bring the machinegun. How could we have done that?" Hailu said. "Anyway General Abebe knows our case. But I hope he will not be in a hurry to raise the issue."

"Why?" Samuel asked.

"He has a lot of time to make a decision."

"What will be your answer for Tegegne's charges if General Abebe raises the question today?"

"We will not give him a reason to raise that question today. If we leave for our camp today promising to return tomorrow, then we will buy time to find people who will plead our case with General Abebe," Hailu suggested lightly.

"What a smart, interesting guy you are!" Samuel said.

Through the fluent ebbs and flow of conversation, the topic of discussion somehow switched from strategy to spouses.

Sergeant Samuel, Hailu and Tadesse eventually decided to go back to camp together. When they reached their assigned camp, they found Kefelew preparing for a journey to General Abebe's camp. Kefelew wanted to carry out the plan Hailu described to Samuel that day.

"Don't forget to mention that you will return by tomorrow morning," said Hailu.

"Don't you forget to tell your relative to inform us about the situation here, that relative of yours...?"

"He has been assigned to serve under General Abebe. So he will get the necessary information," Hailu answered.

The four men went to General Abebe's tent a little nervous, hoping he would grant them their seemingly harmless request.

"I'm afraid General Abebe will raise Tegegne Busera's case when he meets with Kefelew," Tadesse said.

"No, I don't think so; you don't talk about a crisis in times of tribulation."

They stood under a tree and waited for Kefelew to come out. When his meeting with General Abebe finally ended, Kefelew walked out with an agitated countenance. Tadesse and Hailu waited for Kefelew to approach them under the tree. Instead, he simply passed them by as if he had not seen them, giving them the indication that the meeting did not go very well. Nevertheless, Hailu and Tadesse followed him.

"What happened?" Hailu finally asked.

"I told General Abebe that we have to return to our village tonight, and come back early tomorrow morning. As soon as it became he would grant us our wish, his assistant aid-decamp whispered something in his ear. The aid-decamp probably reminded him of our case with Tegegne Busera. General Abebe contemplated for a moment, and then finally said, 'I will expect you tomorrow.' I think General Abebe will court-martial me by tomorrow."

"Anyway we will hear about their plan in the morning. My relative has promised me he will send a messenger late in the night to our camp," Hailu said.

"We will see..."

"It is always simple to go downhill!" advised Tadesse, who was trying to buoy up his friend's spirits by remaining optimistic. They made their journey back to camp in the Adabai lowland after sunset.

In the next day commanders from Menz, Yifat, Tegulet, and senior officers from General Abebe army assembled chaired by General Abebe. Kefelew did not attend the meeting.

"Gentlemen," General Abebe said, "I know Kefelew has become disobedient. There were more important things we should have discussed and solved than Tegegne Busera's machinegun. You all have divided Menz and Tegulet into estate and every partisan leader has forbidden others to come and go to his estate. You have built small sovereign estates which are an obstacle to the overall patriotic war we witnessed when our army came to Menz and Tegulet," General Abebe's voice showed a hint of anger.

"We did it out of concern for the well-being of the peasantry. If the peasants are dissatisfied we will be like a tree without roots," Hailu replied.

"What you said is correct. But how do you protect the peasants with such an unconstructive method?"

"At least the levy they pay will be for a certain contingent and not for all."

"You are forgetting something," General Abebe interrupted before Hailu could explain any further. "They are expected to pay taxes to the government and no one else, regardless of the conditions. This division of territory is only a by-product of a form of patriotic struggle. It only creates anarchy and burdens the peasants with double taxation. You're not helping anyone with this ridiculous idea."

"All commanders including Commander Gizachew accepted General Abebe's recommendation.

3

Kefelew's insubordination towards General Abebe became an issue of concern for the Menz, Tegulet, and Yifat partisans. Gizachew Haile wrote a letter urging Kefelew not to confront General Abebe, not only for his own sake but also for the sake of not giving the enemy material for propaganda. Gizachew also invited Kefelew to come to him and discuss the problem. Last year, the elders of Menz elected Gizachew as Chief Coordinator and Kefelew as Deputy Coordinator of the partisan's struggle. Now the command structure was taking its course under the strength of each partisan group.

However, to Gizachew's dismay, Kefelew refused the invitation, lying about his unfitness to travel due to health problems. Kefelew rather suggested to his followers that he did not want to have a face-to-face meeting with General Abebe, and if forced he would even fight back.

"I don't think there is a place where we can retreat. If we retreat, we should go to Sela Dingay and attack the Italian camp over there. In this case, General Abebe may not order his army to attack us. If we buy time through this means, it may be a way for us to get out of this problem," Hailu suggested.

"We will discuss it in the assembly. You can present your idea there," said Kefelew.

"General Abebe has said that he is offended by the creation of protected areas," said Hailu taking this moment as the right time to present the issue.

"Were you not the one who said that the peasants have to be protected? They chose their protectors," Kefelew rebutted.

Hailu summarized what General Abebe said in the meeting. Hailu admitted that what he suggested earlier was wrong. It was at this time that Gizachew Haile's messenger appeared.

Gizachew Haile's letter was very short. It reiterated that war between brothers would only give happiness to the enemy. In the letter, Gizachew asked Kefelew to come to him for further discussion, or if that was not possible, Gizachew suggested that he could come to Kefelew.

Kefelew responded with a letter declining the invitation due to health reasons and gave no mention of another time or place to meet.

"Let me at least go to Mr. Gizachew Haile, and hear his full intention," pleaded Hailu.

"You can go with all your men. I will face it alone," said Kefelew.

"No, I need only three people to go with me. The affair concerns all of us equally," said Hailu.

"As you wish," Kefelew relented.

Hailu left with three people to Gizachew Haile. Hailu met Gizachew and Gizachew told Hailu to persuade Kefelew not to confront General Abebe. "It would be better if he retreated. Tell him that I am begging him to retreat," Gizachew seemed desperate.

[165]

Hailu returned that night to Kefelew and the next day, they saw from afar General Abebe's army moving towards them.

Kefelew's army retreated. General Abebe's army followed suit. The chase continued for some time, with both men looking at each other through field telescopes from time to time. Then the night descended over the valleys, and the two armies stopped for rest.

Before sunrise, Kefelew's army descended to the Valley of Mofer Wouha River and saw General Abebe's army following it. The two armies, three kilometers from each other, began to ascend the valley on their way to Sela Dingay town, which had been occupied by the Italians the year before.

"Do you remember your promise last year when I saved your life?" asked Hailu.

"Yes. How could I forget it," answered Kefelew.

"Then I want to use that promise today. You can feel assured that you have paid the debt."

"Ok, say it."

"I don't want you to feel bad, and you should believe me completely. I want to go to General Abebe's camp and try to negotiate with him. I do not need people to follow me. My brother Wolde will carry the machinegun and take command of my unit until I return. Will you grant me this and allow me to leave?"

"I will," said Kefelew, after a heavy struggle with his conscience.

Hailu began running the descent down the valley. He was leaping like a monkey from rock to rock, finding the shortest path. He crossed the Mofer Wouha River and began to ascend the mountain.

Suddenly, Hailu heard a man behind him shout, "Hands up and don't look back. You are Kefelew's man. You do not carry a rifle or a strange pistol."

"I am carrying a message to General Abebe. I am in a hurry," Hailu replied.

"That is permissible within our war tradition. Nevertheless, I have a personal grudge against you. You have ill intent towards my wife. I will shoot you like a dog. Don't look back or you are a dead duck."

"I don't know you," said Hailu, being careful how he should handle the situation.

"I know you very well. Turn back your face slowly," said the man.

Hailu turned and looked at Samuel, Meseret's husband, who was laughing his heart out.

"Oh God" said Hailu.

"Well, don't be so careless at this time. If you are going to try mediating then, hurry up!" Samuel said, "Be quick! Already we have received orders to destroy your army."

Hailu quickly left Samuel. He was very tired when he topped the valley and reached General Abebe's camp. He saw Gizachew Haile looking dejected and sad standing with Beshah. He saluted them, bowing from his neck and back in due honor to them in the traditional way of saluting.

"Hailu, welcome," said Gizachew. "What now?"

"We are just retreating. Even we are going to attack the Italian army in Sela Dingay to stop this bloodshed between brothers," said Hailu in great agitation.

"General Abebe was informed that you were going to Sela Dingay to join the Italians. Thus he gave an order for the destruction of your army."

"I have already heard that."

Gizachew looked through his field glasses. He then handed them to Hailu.

Hailu looked through the field glasses at Kefelew's army. They were moving up and the Italian army moved out to meet them fully armed... "I am going back to my friends," Hailu said handing back the field glasses to Gizachew.

"No, you shouldn't. Let's go and talk to General Abebe," said Gizachew.

Gizachew and Hailu stood behind General Abebe without him noticing. General Abebe was looking through his glass and said to Demissie Wolde Amanuel. "Ah! The Italians have already come out welcoming him and protecting him from us. He must have informed them through letters that he has betrayed us!"

"Excuse me, Your Excellency. We are just moving up to attack the Italians," said Hailu.

General Abebe looked at him then at Gizachew Haile.

"Do you also support his insubordination and anarchistic behavior?" asked an agitated General Abebe.

"No. We are just in a dilemma. I am suggesting the need to follow an alternative strategy," said Gizachew.

"We have already studied a better solution," said Demissie Wolde Amanuel. He was part of one of the active intelligentsia groups within the partisan movement. As such, General Abebe usually consults Demissie for strategic and tactical advice. His intelligence and perceptive ideas were unparalleled within the ranks of the partisans.

"Send a messenger to the front commanders and cancel the war order!" General Abebe said. Demissie ran out and then returned.

"What was your solution, gentleman?" asked General Abebe

"It is the establishment of an association of partisan leaders throughout the country," Demissie Wolde Amanuel explained. "The signing of the rules and regulations of the Association by all military commanders will render formal constitution and legality. If there was such an association, we would have been able to punish and to excommunicate stubborn elements such as Kefelew." Then Demissie Wolde Amanuel continued to lecture on legal theories, citing examples from the experiences of European leaders and at last from the first constitution of Ethiopia.

"Well, what do you think about this?" General Abebe asked Gizachew Haile.

"This is a very good idea. It will help to bring all the partisans in the provinces under a unified command.

"Well then Demissie, discuss it with your friends and prepare the Articles of the Association," said General Abebe and ordered the cancellation of the previous order for attacking Kefelew's army.

The transmission of the new order through coded machine-gun fires started. The second front returned fire to verify it has accepted the message and transmitted it to the third contingent. Samuel's contingent, to verify it has accepted the message, began to transmit the counter-message.

"The Italians must have thought that we are firing at each other. They are dancing while looking at us," said Hailu, still looking through the field glass. "Oh! My friends are going down to Akre."

"They also have an intelligence unit. But it is so lacking that it might not have deciphered our signals yet," said Demissie, not hearing what Hailu just said.

"I want to go to my units. See you later," said Hailu bowing from his back, and then began to descend the escarpment. "You have ill intent to my wife." The words of Samuel began to repeat themselves in his ears. "Why was he joking in such a way? She is pregnant isn't she?" he asked himself. Then he tried to forget all about it. However, the words were still ringing in his ears, and he was repeating them silently.

He reached Akre in the early night and then reported to Kefelew. Kefelew felt happy. Hailu went to his assigned place and fell asleep. He fell into a deep sleep and when he awoke several hours later, it was lunchtime. A messenger approached him. "What happened?" asked Hailu in a dejected, drowsy tone, still trying to wake up.

"General Abebe has decided to confine Kefelew in the valley," the messenger said.

"For what?"

"I think for insubordination."

Hailu smiled and asked him about the progress of the new association planned to be organized.

"Everybody has accepted the idea as very good. General Abebe has already ordered the foreign-educated people to prepare letters to summon partisans from all over Ethiopia for a meeting on October 23, 1939 at the prairie above Meseret's grandmother home, Nib Washa.

General Abebe with his army left to Jiru.

After 3 days, General Abebe's invitation letter for all partisan leaders to attend the first meeting for the formation of Ancient Ethiopia's Heroes Association reached Kefelew in Akre. There were four months until October. Kefelew read it thoroughly then asked Hailu for his opinion.

"What do you suggest?"

"This may be a way out of our problem," said Hailu, who was also happy about the letter that renewed his friendship with Kefelew. "Let's call a meeting of the partisans and discuss it."

"We will discuss it when the time comes."

4

The meeting of the partisans began fifteen days before the commencement of the conference to establish Ancient Ethiopia's Heroes Association for October 23, 1939. Kefelew read the invitation letter written two months earlier. The letter signed by General Abebe invited Kefelew to represent his partisan movement in the planned conference. The conference aimed to establish an association of patriots to strengthen cooperation. Through the association, they plan to record the exploits of the patriots so that their exemplary deeds would be a guide for posterity.

"I think this is a good idea," said one partisan, with whom many agreed.

"I would not be able to represent you in the meeting. These days I feel ill, so I don't want to go," said Kefelew.

"It is better if you try."

"We may as well elect another representative. I think Hailu will do," said Kefelew confirming his intention of not attending the meeting.

"General Abebe may be offended. This will also create a problem for us," advised one of the group.

"We will only find a way out of this dilemma if Kefelew would be willing to sign the agreement and then come back. His absence may be falsely interpreted as a reflection of our rebellious leanings," Hailu said.

"That is a good suggestion. Nevertheless, we know that Kefelew will not capitulate. So it is better if he writes a letter stating that he is sick and giving you the authorization to represent our group," said the pragmatic priest.

Hailu left for Ankelafigne one day before the day of the meeting. He passed by the house of Meseret's grandmother and immediately remembered what Samuel jokingly told him a few days ago, "You covet my wife. I will kill you." The words began to hammer through his ears as if a constant drumbeat. "It is nothing. It is a simple joke. I should not think about it. Better to admire this endless plain," he mused. Months had passed since the last time he crossed this same grassland plain with wounded compatriots from Bulga. Below the plain, Hailu saw the remnants of Taitu's magnificent mansion, destroyed by Italian bombardment.

He passed an elevated land amidst the plain and looked towards the chain of mountains on the horizon. He identified the village of Samuel's father and remembered what Samuel had told him about his father, that he owned a vast stretch of farmland in his village. Hailu reminisced on the one time he saw Samuel's father in Addis Ababa during the campaign to Maichew. He sat on a white horse, with four people with rifles following him along with twenty others armed with sticks and spears.

Incidentally, the first two people he met in Ankelafigne were Samuel and Meseret. Hailu greeted Samuel warmly but looked down when he greeted Meseret, "How do you do?" Hailu coyly said to Meseret without looking at her.

"So you came. It means Kefelew refused to come. General Abebe will be angry," commented Samuel.

"Kefelew is sick. General Abebe will understand," Hailu said, hoping his words were true.

"The excuse is very weak as a reason for disobedience," Samuel said.

"It is better to hope for the best," Meseret interjected.

Samuel's analysis proved to be correct. General Abebe allowed Hailu only to sign for his units and said, "We will wait for Kefelew to be well enough to sign the document in the name of his followers," said General Abebe making it clear that he took Kefelew's absence as disruptive.

Ancient Ethiopia's Heroes Association's first General Meeting where Ethiopian patriotic army representatives from the whole of Ethiopia participated opened in the vast prairie above

Meseret's grandmother Taitu's, house. Hailu participated as a representative of Kefelew and his army.

The Association's General Assembly elected General Abebe as its first president. With the establishment of the Ancient Ethiopia's Patriotic Association, the renowned strategist General Abebe became the coordinator of the Ethiopian patriotic armies.

The General's strategy of tens of thousands of soldiers farming during the winter seasons, serving as scouts looking for the enemies every day, and assembling around their commanders in their thousands to conduct conventional battles when called upon made him famous. His fame reached as far as Europe and China.

General Amoraw Woubeneh invited the participants to attend the next meeting in Gojjam; and the assembly gladly accepted the offer. Others were putting in their bids for the subsequent meetings in Harar, Tigrai, Wollega, and Kaffa. General Abebe thanked all for their offers and said to them, "I hope we will conduct our yearly meetings in the near future with freedom and independence."

The next day, General Abebe left to Bulga and the other representatives of the patriotic armies returned to their respective provinces. Kefelew was fortunate to have a few days's respite, but Hailu was sure General Abebe would not forget his absence.

In sheer frustration, the Italians started terrorist attacks aimed at assassinating of patriotic leaders using paid mercenaries from the localities. Rumors were rife that in all provinces traitors were assassinating patriotic leaders.

"Italy, she love-a da justice! You sell- a me Haile Selassie an' I sell a you Franco-yes?"

Prospect of a deal by David Low, 1937

Part Seven: War and Love
Meseret/Samuel

1

Meseret was getting ready for the journey back to Bulga with her husband Samuel along with Beshah's army when her husband asked her "Meseret, you are nine months pregnant. Do you think you can make it to Bulga?"

She answered that she could. He tried to reason with her. He promised her that he would return from Bulga if she waited for him at his parents' residence, which was nearby on the left side of the Gorge. But Meseret refused.

Samuel compromised and they started their journey to Bulga. They had not covered two kilometers when she felt terrible pain and settled on the grass.

"What is it Meseret?" Samuel asked, concerned for his wife's welfare.

"Well. If Mahlet was here..."

"I got news about her. She was still in the Sasit Italian camp. She is a prisoner, yes, but she is doing fine."

Meseret winced in pain. "It must be a contraction. Please call the midwife," Meseret demanded in agony.

Samuel ran to the village and returned with the midwife. "Oh God protect us," he cried.

Meseret gave birth to a son before they left Ankelafigne, in the prairie land above the home of Sergeant Samuel's parents.

Commander Beshah congratulated Meseret and Samuel and ordered Samuel to take her and the child to his parent's home nearby and meet him after a while in Bulga.

Samuel, with his two men, quickly carried Meseret and his newborn son on a stretcher down the Mofer Wouha River.

"Meseret, we will call our child Meshageria (Bridge)," said Samuel walking beside the stretcher.

"Why?"

"Well, Meseret, a new era has dawned. The base of our society is eroding, even though it seems intact. The gap between the people is widening. Some are going down the economic ladder while others are rising to the top."

Meseret listened intently.

"Take Argaw Benebiru. He was a tenant working for his landlord. In the past years as a partisan he has become master of a district. He even imprisons and maltreats the feudal lords who were once his superiors. Kefelew was a son of a lawyer, but currently his power extends all over Menz. Take Hailu, who was he before this war? He was a simple private soldier under me. He has become someone feared in the Adabai Gorge, an economically and militarily powerful partisan leader where his wishes have become the law of the district he governs. All the lords and chiefs, except for a few, have gone down the ladder. The traditional lords and chiefs have lost their powers and rights."

"I don't believe it," Meseret dismissed what her husband observed as truth.

"I don't expect you to. You are going with the tides. Your class status is still intact."

"Why do you want our child to be called Meshageria?"

"From this era, we will pass to another era when we will gain our freedom. We may not see the day of independence. But through our child, we will be a part of the era that dawns."

"God's will is not predictable."

"Meseret when my child is baptized, I want to host a big feast."

"How will that be possible?"

"I will find a way."

"Ok," said Meseret, not wanting to hurt his feelings.

They spent some weeks in the house of Samuel's father. Samuel's family was happy to take care of Meseret and nurse her child. The whole village viewed Meseret and Samuel as the ideal couple.

Meseret and the other wives of the partisans were ideal companions. The partisans' wives were doubly burdened during this time of crisis by the responsibility of raising their children and boosting up the morale of their husbands. Sometimes, after a disheartening defeat, they would sing war songs to their husbands to raise their spirits to prepare them for their next battle. At other times, they would take care of the household chores, like food and laundry, so that their husbands could focus on the grueling mission that lay ahead. In addition, in times of conflict amongst the partisans they would tactfully mitigate any differences between brothers. Samuel took a moment to appreciate his wife and everything she had been through on his behalf.

2

After spending a few weeks with Meseret in his parent's house, Samuel felt the need to go to his battalion. "Meseret you need to spend a few months here. I have to go to the main army. On my way to your uncle Commander Beshah I need to console the family of a deceased patriot."

"I can come with you. I will not remain here alone," Meseret insisted. He begged her to stay with his parents and care for their child. She was helpless in the face of his plea and conceded.

Samuel left with his men, leaving his wife and the newborn son behind.

Meseret felt lonely. This was their first time of separation from one another since becoming a couple. As a result, the ensuing days were long and difficult for Meseret; even though Samuel's parents did everything they could to make her feel comfortable. Meseret lived life of a recluse when separated from her one true love, Samuel.

Then, one day while she was nursing her child, she heard a voice reverberate through the mountains, a sign that something bad had happened or was about to happen. She became nervous.

She went out of the house and stood with the villagers, trying to decipher the message. A man standing beside Meseret yelled out, "We cannot hear you!"

Another man, who heard the message clearly, rang out, "He is saying someone has died. Does anyone know someone who was sick beyond there?" he asked, pointing in the distance from where the voice echoed. People talked to each other in vain.

At last, all heard the message. "Samuel has been wounded. He is in Sasit." Meseret's knees buckled; she felt as if the ground swept from under her feet. Then she composed herself and began to climb to the prairie above Ilqoya. The villagers followed her. She then looked back and said, "Fathers, mothers, sisters, this is not a death call. I only want to bring my husband back. Only three or four equestrians will follow me. The rest of you, I beg you to remain behind," she said, trying to fight back tears.

"That is impossible," said an old man, many murmured in agreement.

"Meseret is right," said the priest.

Meseret mounted the horse and left with three equestrians. The three equestrians followed her. A soldier who was with Samuel came galloping towards them. He told her that his friends were searching for the culprits all the way to Debre Birhan, assuming they would run to the Italian camp. Meseret without a word rode towards the escarpment, rather than the middle of the prairie, which was a short distance from Sasit. Four equestrians, one of which was the priest, followed her. Meseret saw three men galloping from the prairie towards the gorge. Meseret and her friends galloped and tried to close in on them. She aimed her gun and shot one of the culprits. He went down with his horse. Two of the culprits fired back and missed Meseret, but one of her companions fell down. She ordered one of her followers to look after the wounded friend and pursued with the priest and another equestrian following her. The two culprits galloped a while then separated. One took the direction of Debre Birhan and the other to the escarpment. Meseret thought that the one who was galloping towards Debre Birhan was the one who shot Samuel. She followed him. The priest and the other equestrians followed her, not wanting to leave her alone. Meseret and her friends came nearer to the rider. He shot at her again but missed. She fired and he fell from his horse. The horse continued to run.

Meseret climbed down from the horse, went forward aiming the gun to his head. The culprit started to plea. "I am not the one who shot Sergeant Samuel. It was Bekele."

"Who is Bekele?" she asked him.

"He is not from this area. He is the one who rode to the gorge."

"Both of you are traitors." She did not wait to hear his response she shot him and turned back to climb her horse.

"Meseret this is enough. We will find the culprit tomorrow. He will not be able to reach the Italian camp. You should go and meet Samuel." It took the priest time to convince her. Then she started to cry, climbed her horse, and galloped to Sasist where Sergeant Samuel was waiting.

They reached Sasit before sunrise. Meseret saw him sitting upright supported by two men on either side. He smiled when he saw his wife. She kissed his cheeks, her face still wet with tears. "How did it happen?" she asked at last.

"Samuel was in this hut. He was playing and chatting with us, laughing, having a good time. Then a bastard traitor shot him in his chest through a hole in the hut."

"Do you know who?" she asked sobbing. She tried to verify the information passed to her by the dead traitor.

"He disappeared into the night."

"I will find him; even his mother's womb won't be a hiding place for him," said Meseret.

"How do you feel?" she asked Samuel when they were alone.

"I feel tired... please move me back and let me stretch...yes.... its ok. Ouch.., it's ok."

"Does it hurt much?"

"A little," he said and asked her to sit by his side and hold his hand."

She held back her tears and tried to smile. She held his hand and looked at him. He was becoming pale. "Please don't," she begged him.

His eyes opened, and he tried to smile. "Meseret," he said in a weak voice that seemed to emanate from a distant place.

"Yes my dear, my lord, what can I do for you," she said facing his defeat and love from his voice.

"Take care of our child... even if," he passed out before he could finish his sentence.

"Oh! Lord," she cried. She wept and whispered, "I beg you, please!" He seemed to hear her plea. She moved her hand over his chest and feet and felt them growing cold. She screamed.

He opened his eyes." He started to speak in agony. "Meseret... our struggle is hard .... You are a woman.... do not forget me.... but you .... You can remarry... You must..."

She called him loudly. He was not responding. She raised her head from his chest and looked at his wooden face. She could not believe it. He was dead.

By the next hour, people carried Samuel's body on a stretcher and began the journey to his father's house at Ilqoya.

People from faraway places started journey to Sergeant Samuel's father residence. They were informed about the sad happening by signals sent from atop the mountain chains.

The next day, Sergeant Samuel's coffin rested on a bed in the field. Around it stood the women on one side and the men on the other in a semi-circle. Meseret and Samuel's relatives were next to the bed crying, while partisans, relatives, friends, and villagers looked upon the lifeless body of a hero.

In honor of a brave soldier, rifles were fired, war songs were sung and flags have flown at half-mast.

All gathered from every direction and formed units in the North, South, East, and West. Meseret was weeping and hearing the singing voices. The voice from the north was clear.

"*Was it not Samuel that killed hundreds of fascist Italians?*
Samuel's rifle has an eye;
The bullet from it never misses an enemy."

A man was singing war songs. The people around him were chanting in unison, moving their rifles over their heads and stamping the ground with their feet.

"Ahoy!" the people said

Then the man increased the tempo of the rhythm and he sang,

"Brave man! Oh, brave man!
Raise my brave man!"

"Ahoy!"

"You brave man! Oh, you brave!"

"Hay, hay, hay, oh, you brave man!"

Chanting their war songs, the people from the four corners of the region reached the field and joined the people who came up from the valley.

The men on one side and the women on the other formed a big circle. The men hoisted a green, yellow, and red flag. The topless women tied their hand-woven scarves around their breasts, pulling and covering their breasts to their chests. Samuel's best friend tied a white band around his forehead; holding his spear with his left hand from which a shield dangled, and a bamboo stick in his right hand and started a war song. Four patriots followed his step as he moved to chant the song of the brave. When he finished, the women in unison chanted, "He has spoken the truth," while they hit their chests with their palms in rhythm. The men pointed their rifles to the sky and fired. Another brave man began his war song in praise of Samuel, mentioning the battlefronts where two of them had fought together. The women stopped chanting to allow the man to speak uninterrupted and silently moving up and down in rhythm to continue honoring Samuel. Next, a brave man spoke ferociously about Samuel's past deeds. He emphatically promised to avenge Sergeant Samuel. The men shot their rifles towards the sky.

The ceremony continued for some time.

Four longhaired partisans raised the bed where the deceased Samuel lay covered with shama, as smoke from the priest's incense holder permeated the air.

When they reached the church compound, the people formed a circle and began to sing their war songs again, still mourning heavily.

The partisans carried Samuel's body into the church while the war songs and rifle shots continued. The church bell rang.

The men and women cried, jumping and shaking their bodies. The rifle shots became intense.

When the ceremony ended, Meseret began to walk down the hill without looking back. Then she felt a tap on her shoulder. She turned around and saw a group of soldiers standing behind her. They were Samuel's soldiers. "Farewell good people. You are free to join the other partisan leaders," she said.

"No." said one of them. "We will follow you. You are our commander now."

She looked in turn at each of them. They were serious. "Oh! A woman as commander," she mused.

They began to ascend the mountain together, and all Meseret could think about was avenging her husband's death. A person who came from the gorge had told her that a stranger had come to the area. She suspected that the person might be the one who killed her husband. She mobilized her soldiers and traveled to the place during the night. They circled the home where the suspected person dwelt and she sent one of her soldiers camouflaged as a peasant to the home, asking for food and water. The head of the household opened the gate and he gave the guest water and some food. The soldier tried to identify the members of the household. A person came and joined him. He told them that he has come from Addis Ababa. The soldier returned and informed Meseret about the case. She entered the home with her soldiers and interviewed the person. She was convinced that the person was not the killer. The head of the household knew Meseret and he offered them his hospitality. They spent the night and in the morning returned to Ilqoya.

After her return from the gorge, she was not feeling well. She complained about a severe headache.

One day, Meseret heard a message ring through the mountains. The message stated that an Italian hireling assassinated Gizachew Haile, the leader of the Menz, Yifat, and Tegulet patriots. The news caused Meseret to faint, sending her into a coma for some time. She remained that way for two weeks. She had contracted malaria. Meseret was given wood brought from Yifat to chew as medicine. She was very weak. The root was crushed, mixed with water, and she was forced to drink it. It took her very long to gain full consciousness.

Gizachew was mourned in both General Abebe's camp and among his compatriots in Menz, Yifat, and Tegulet. Many remembered his famous speech to his soldiers about stretching one's hand and touching the sky, while he had been lying wounded in the battle in the North four years earlier.

While Meseret was delirious, the patriots took serious and extreme measures against all the traitors and hirelings in the region, one of whom was Samuel's assailant. A partisan whispered the good news to Meseret while she was still semi-conscious.

"Your husband has been avenged." He hoped she would hear him.

Gizachew Haile was also avenged. The traitors were found and killed without mercy.

3

Meseret opened her eyes and found herself sleeping in a cave. Beside her was her sister and best friend, Mahlet, who had escaped from the Italian internment. Mahlet dipped a spoon in a bowl of wheat and barley syrup, and then fed Meseret. "This must be a dream," Meseret said in a faint voice.

"Yes, it is a dream. You are getting better," answered Mahlet, without much thought. Then she kissed Meseret's forehead.

Meseret grabbed Mahlet's hands and said, "Let it not be a dream."

"It is not a dream."

"Where am I?"

You were sick for the last month. You had malaria but you are now recovering."

"How did you come here?" Meseret asked, still unsure whether she was dreaming or awake.

"Your soldiers were fighting daily when they transported you here. The people with the Italians were talking about you in the camp. I heard that you were sick, so I escaped and came here."

"Thank God," Meseret said and pulled Mahlet towards her. She kissed her cheeks and then began to cry. When Mahlet saw Meseret crying she became aware of how emotionally vulnerable her sister had become.

Soon after, Meseret recovered. The reason for such a fast recovery was puzzling. Perhaps Mahlet's presence created the magic or the death of the person who killed her husband. Either way, all the partisans were happy to see their new leader healthy enough to continue the liberation struggle.

Meseret and Mahlet found time to sit together and catch up with recent events.

"How are the Italian barbarians in their social life?" Meseret asked Mahlet.

Mahlet smiled, and then answered, "They are very lusty. One of the Ethiopians who work with them told me that the Mussolini, their king, promised them that Ethiopian women with big breasts would be their property."

"Do they rape our women in prison?"

"Yes sometimes. When an Italian sees a woman that he likes, he will force her to go to bed with him. They are real barbarians."

"How do the raped women continue after they are freed?"

"They go to the Kahn and tell what happened and then they drink and wash with holy waters for fifteen days and reemerge cleansed."

Both kept quiet for a while.

"The Italians also perform tasks, which take us years in a few days. They make the devil assist them in their duties."

"How do they tame the devil?" Meseret wondered.

"I don't know. Their cars are made of iron. It must be imprisoned somewhere in the iron cage."

"Oh God"

Her understanding of the Italian ways and tactics made Mahlet a sought-after adviser for the partisans.

Meseret, at last, decided to move to Bulga and hand over Samuel's army to her uncle, Commander Beshah, and concentrate on nursing her child. Mahlet and Samuel's soldiers agreed. They traveled to Bulga, avoiding the Italian garrison towns.

When she reached General Abebe's camp, he received her with great honor and admiration.

"Well my lady, you came at last as a hero, intact with the army. It is a great deed. The soldiers would have dispersed and it would have been a great loss. Now they come intact. We have been rewarded for what we lost in the death of our great fighter Sergeant Samuel."

Meseret turned her eyes to the earth in satisfaction.

"Commander Beshah will come here soon. He will be proud of you."

She went from General Abebe to the other camps and waited for her uncle Beshah. He came, kissed her cheeks and looking at her in great love and admiration with his stuttering speech at last said, "What should I call you?"

"This is your second time asking me such a question. Does it need an answer?"

"No," Beshah smiled. "I just wanted to express how proud I am of you."

"Thank you. By the way, I want to go to Samuel's father's house tomorrow," Meseret said.

"Why? The Italians will be enraged when they hear that you have turned over Samuel's army to us. Even they will send their assassins," said Commander Beshah in deep concern.

"Everything happens when God has willed it. My priority is to look after Samuel's son and mine."

Commander Beshah saw in her the determination that he had observed when she first came to join the army three years earlier in Sasit, but he could not help but emphasize the security issue. "You know Meseret, when they killed Samuel, they expected his army to fall apart."

"Anyway, I will leave with two of my soldiers and they will be sufficient to protect me and my son."

The next day, she returned to Ilqoya, Samuel's father's village. Afterward, she went underground with her son, Mahlet and her two soldiers, to avoid mercenary assassins.

"Oh God, what a lonely lady," said Hailu after he heard of Samuel's death, the heroic acts of Meseret and the honor she received from General Abebe and now her disappearance in the underground.

Part Eight: War and Destiny
Hailu

1

Kefelew and Hailu, along with their armies, returned to Quatch after the culmination of the first General Assembly, which had established Ancient Ethiopia's Heroes Association.

On the way to Quatch, they rested on a cliff. Hailu looked at the Adabai River below. He felt a thrill. The Adabai seemed to go back, but it still flowed forward. Hailu knew that the Adabai flowed in a southeastern direction, and not in the direction that it appeared to flow, northeastern. "Why don't we hurry down to the Adabai?" Hailu suggested.

"Why do we have to hurry?"

"A monkey and a partisan always like their cliffs. They feel at home there. One who resides on top of mountains is only a scout."

"Do you see how things are changing Hailu?" asked Wolde one day in Quatch.

"What is changing?"

"Look at Tesema Irgete. The person who once commanded thousands of soldiers, currently has only a few followers," said his brother. "Beshah faced the same problem. The number of his soldiers has dwindled after he moved to Bulga far from his home base in Tegulet."

"Yes. But have you heard anything about Meseret, Samuel's widow?" Hailu asked, remembering her with the mention of Beshah, her uncle.

"It is said she only remains with two soldiers. She has gone underground. She may come to Nib Washa, her childhood village. Hailu, Nib Washa is under your administration," said Wolde, smiling.

"It will be a great honor for me to serve her. I remember Sergeant Samuel her husband. He was a good person, a gallant fighter and an excellent commander," said Hailu remembering the time they spent together during the campaign to the northern war fronts four years earlier.

Meseret's whereabouts remained a secret for a while. Then news came that she has settled with her grandmother Taitu in Nib Washa. Meseret and her soldiers earlier were in a cave near Ilqoya, the birthplace of her late husband Sergeant Samuel. Ilqoya was only a four-hour journey from Nib Washa

"My friends," said Hailu to his soldiers, "we have to help fellow patriots. Meseret has come to an area under our control. We should contribute something that will help the deceased Samuel's child and widow," Hailu suggested.

The partisans each contributed enough money to buy a cow. Hailu, as a representative of the partisan group was to take and hand over the cow to Meseret. He was happy to be chosen for such an errand.

2

Meseret and Mahlet were discussing their escape from the Italian encirclement of the previous week while they were on their way to Nib Washa, the village where both of them grew up. For the time being, they dwelt in a cave to avoid Italian capture. "It was just a miracle we came out of it," said Mahlet, remembering how narrowly they had escaped being targeted by mercenary assassins.

"Let God's will be done. No one dies before God's appointed time," Meseret said.

"Does God also interfere in such affairs?" asked Mahlet.

"Yes everything is predetermined. You can ask our priest. He told me himself."

"Let him preserve us," Mahlet said.

"Let his wishes be done."

Meseret looked through a hole in the cave and saw armed soldiers approaching her. "How do they know our whereabouts," Meseret mused. "They must have betrayed me, those mercenaries. Our own type," she moved to the corner where her rifle was. Her feet felt heavy, but she knew she could not show her fear as Mahlet does. Meseret was the leader.

At that moment, Meseret's scout entered the cave. Meseret aimed her rifle at him and said, "You scoundrel. Don't move! You betrayed me."

"No my sister, I came here only with friends. They are Hailu and his friends coming to show their respect to you according to the principles of Ancient Ethiopian Heroes Association."

"Why didn't you inform me in advance?" she asked

"I was mistaken. Forgive me," the scout said, with his hands in the air.

"Show them to me," she said, putting down her rifle.

"How are you?" said Hailu entering the cave with two of his companions.

"I am fine. Bless God. How are you?" she said

"Today is one year since our comrade Sergeant Samuel was martyred. In remembrance, our battalion sent us to show respect in all their names," he said and stood silently.

Meseret cordially asked him to sit on a stone near the cave wall.

He sat motionlessly. His friends were also quiet. Meseret made a fire and prepared coffee. He looked at her glowing eyes and her graceful posture. "How can a person imagine this lady will lead soldiers in a battle front?" he thought.

After the coffee, Hailu rose up and said, "Our units have sent a cow to be milked for the son of the deceased."

"I am very grateful for your help. Please thank all your units in the name of my son and myself. I will be grateful if you send the cow to Samuel's family home."

"You deserve it. We should have helped you much more."

"Hailu has also brought personally a quintal of grain," said Mahlet.

"Thank you," Meseret said.

Hailu and his men bowed their heads, and then they left.

Meseret turned to the fireplace and began to scratch the ash with a piece of wood. Mahlet came and sat beside her. Then Mahlet asked, "Meseret, why don't you marry Hailu?"

"What?" Meseret asked angrily.

"Well, you know that Samuel also willed that you should get married."

"So what"

"Meseret, our female family members have never married their choice. Their elders, for whatever reason they saw fit, decided whom they should marry."

"Please keep quiet," said Meseret, her anger visible on her face.

Mahlet left and Meseret remained near the fireplace. Moments later, Meseret stepped outside and saw Hailu and his men walking down the gorge. A fleeting thought of marrying Hailu entered her mind, but it quickly dissipated. She shook her head, went back inside to go to bed. It had been a long day.

3

Hailu and his friend seemed very happy. They had accomplished what a living friend should perform in memory of his fallen comrade.

"Hailu look over there. Tesema Irgete with his followers is coming this way."

Hailu looked at them. "Where were they?" he mused. He stood and waited for them. Tesema Irgete who had commanded thousands of soldiers currently commands only five soldiers. Hailu, remembering the former glory of

Tesema, showed his deference. "Good afternoon my sir," he saluted Tesema Irgete.

"Good afternoon," said Tesema Irgete. "Have you visited Meseret, my relative?"

"Yes."

"I was trying to find her, but I was not lucky. I came here to ask you if you know of her whereabouts?" asked Tesema.

Hailu told him her whereabouts. "I will visit her some other day. It is already late," said Tesema. "Have you heard the new song?" He asked smiling.

"What song?"

Tesema cleared his throat and hitting the ground in turn with his two feet and moving his shoulders and hands left and right in the traditional dance, sang the song.

Abebe Aregai says to us,
  Compromise with them;
Who will be the peace brokers?
  When there are no intermediaries;
Between the Italians and the Ethiopians.

He then laughed.

"Where did you get that song?" Hailu sadly asked.

"Someone sang it to us on our way here."

"I don't think it mocks General Abebe. I met a friend of mine a week ago who came from General Abebe. He briefed me on the situation."

"Go on then, tell us what he said," Tesema seemed very curious.

"He said that information has reached General Abebe that the Italians are going to war with Great Britain, Russia, and America."

"Is that true?" someone asked.

"Yes, it seems so. Even Tekle, our secret agent in Addis Ababa, has written a letter to Kefelew to this effect," Hailu added.

"Well if the Italians are in a mess, why don't we just drive them out of our lands?" asked Tesema.

"The Italians asked for a compromise because they are standing on fire," Hailu declared. "They want to make a big concession to the partisans to transfer their soldiers to British Somaliland, Sudan and North Africa front to engage the British, who have been assigned by the allies to oust them."

"Then?" someone interjected.

"Let me finish." Hailu continued. "General Abebe thought that if we remain weak in the new situation even the British would replace the Italians. Therefore, he is trying to be farsighted. If the Ethiopian armies strengthened themselves, then we could negotiate from a position of strength with the British when they defeat the Italians."

"What if the Italians defeat the British?"

"That is impossible, as the learned people with General Abebe have analyzed it, Britain is very powerful. It is said that Emperor Haile Selassie has also written to General Abebe about the coming war," Hailu said.

"What are the terms for compromise?" Tesema asked.

"The Italians have made clear their terms through papers they distributed to the Ethiopian army and the population. They promised to reinstate the traditional rulers and chieftains, give due recognition to the culture and religion of the people. They want to hand over even their military camps if an agreement for armistice is signed. They are retreating their positions because they want to transfer their armies to fight the British and in recognition of their failures to settle Italian colonizers in Ethiopia," argued Hailu.

"Does the compromise include us?" someone asked.

"I am not sure."

They reached their village and dispersed to their assigned places. The next morning it was St. Gabriel's festival at Keya. The patriots left Wolde as a scout and headed for their villages.

On their way to Keya, they encountered a small Italian unit. They engaged in battle and the Italian army unit retreated. Kefelew and Hailu suspected that the Italians were losing the war and faced problems. This led them to discuss Tekle, the head of the secret service in Addis Ababa.

"He was expected to arrive yesterday. But he didn't show up."

They continued their journey and reached Keya Gabriel.

For the yearly festival of St. Gabriel, the tabot, a replica of the Ark of the Covenant, was carried around the surrounding fields by a priest who had fasted for two days. The partisans, singing war songs, followed the tabot and the priests. The tabot rounded the church and returned to its seat amidst cries of happiness and rifle shots. Then the people in Keya gave a great feast to all who came from the surrounding regions.

The following day, Kefelew insisted that they return to their place in Quatch. When they reached Quatch, a partisan assigned to Wolde came to Kefelew and Hailu and reported that the scouts overwhelmed by a large army had retreated west.

"Another man is hurrying from Keya," said Hailu.

The man saluted and reported. "A big Italian army is moving in this direction."

Tens of thousands of Italian soldiers surrounded them. The annihilation of this partisan contingent seemed imminent.

4

A meeting of commanders headed by Kefelew gathered to decide on appropriate strategies to break the enemy's encirclement. Hailu waited for his turn to air his ideas. His turn came. Hailu stood up confidently and said, "Yesterday we celebrated St. Gabriel. This day with God's help, we shall break the Italian encirclement during the night and pass to Afkera, where, with a few more people, we could maintain defense for a longer duration of time. Afkera is a natural fortification. From there we will push back the enemy and get rid of these barbarian invaders," he recommended.

"Go on," said Kefelew encouraging Hailu to expound his tactics.

"We will follow the river bed, and then at night, we will engage in a battle to break the encirclement, with the aid of Saint Gabriel, our Patron Angel, of course."

"We have never fought during the night before. It may be difficult for us," one partisan said.

"Hailu has formal military training. He may be acquainted with it," said Kefelew.

"Let's agree with Hailu's proposal. He is more familiar with the grounds since he grew up here," another partisan agreed.

Through consensus, Hailu took the assignment to direct the units with the rules of night fighting.

"We have to move to the river in the middle of the night. We must not fire a single rifle shot. We must only use hand grenades. Rifle shots will indicate our whereabouts to the Italians. This is an absolute necessity," Hailu demanded.

"What will we do if they fire at us?" asked one.

"We will remain calm and move swiftly," Hailu replied.

"Let's review the plans," said Kefelew. "Mekuria and fifty of his soldiers will be in the forefront followed by Hailu with a total force of 400. Other commanders will be responsible for carrying equipment and supplies. They will follow Hailu. The rearguard will be directed by me."

When Hailu left the meeting, his village people met him. He saw the old, the young, and the children. He felt deeply sad for them. He went to them, and after greeting them, he gave them advice. "When the Italians occupied the territory, tell them that the so-called partisan thieves have forced you to serve them. Do not feel ashamed. It is a tactic. Tell them and pretend as if you consider them your liberators."

"How could we do that?" asked the elder.

"Why should you be frank with the barbarians anyway?"

"True," said the elder. "We should accept Hailu's advice. God bless you, Hailu."

"Then all of you agree?" Hailu asked them.

"Yes, but the children may leak our secrets."

"My mothers and elders let me tell you something. Children are wise little people. If you advise them in earnest, they can make miracles." Hailu said goodbye to them and told them to pass his advice on to all.

In the moonless night, the encircled partisans moved quietly, forming wide semicircles in all rows. If a partisan wanted to communicate with another, he would make a clicking sound by clapping his tongue to his larynx. In this way, the partisans could communicate to one another without being detected by the Italians. Partisans in the first row could check and listen to the partisans in the last row.

Someone in the first row of Hailu's group made the clicking sound. He did not hear a response, and so told his compatriot beside him, "I don't hear a reply, do you?"

"No, I do not either," said the other in bewilderment.

The two men made the clicking sound together. This was a call for the scouts. The scouts responded. "Do you hear footsteps from partisan brothers in the first row?" he asked the scout.

"No," answered the scout. Then he moved forward to check on the first row's whereabouts. To his surprise, the scout did not see the first row contingent at all. "We should inform Hailu immediately." The scout quickly moved to the middle row.

"Hailu, the whereabouts of the first group led by Mekuria is unknown," said the scout.

"Why don't you go forward and check," Hailu suggested.

"I did."

Hailu, followed by two other people, went forward and entered the riverbed. He lighted a flashlight on the stones and trailed in a northern direction.

At one spot, he saw the wet stones. He felt that his friends might have lost their way and at the same time, he became suspicious that they might have defected to the Italians. He returned to his group and stationed his partisans on the right track. Then, he sent Kefelew a message. To be courteous he said, "The first group is not to be found in its assigned place." Then he waited for a reply.

Kefelew came and asked Hailu, "Where did they disappear?"

"Their footprints show to the northern direction."

"That means my uncle Mekuria has defected to the Italians," Kefelew said in despair.

Hailu kept quiet.

"My unit could take the responsibility of a vanguard," said Kefelew.

"No. Since the first row has disappeared, I will be in the first row," said Hailu.

"Remember I will be close to you at any time," said Kefelew.

Hailu simply shook his head. He had a melancholy countenance. "How could Mekuria do such a thing," he thought to himself.

The partisans continued their movement. When Hailu's group reached the riverbed that lead to Afkera, he called with a clicking sound and assembled his soldiers. He whispered directions to them. "Now do not forget that you must not shoot a rifle. Only use hand grenades at the appointed moment. Remember that you must not shoot even if they fire at you. Please move cautiously. During the night, your footsteps are audible from afar. Be as agile as a cat."

They moved down the cliff to the river. Then Hailu met with Kefelew for the second time. "Why did you leave your position?" asked Hailu.

"Hailu, my uncle has left me. We have to make a formal promise to one another to never abandon each other."

"Agreed," said Hailu. "We are brothers."

"Amen," Kefelew said, and then returned to his position.

When they reached the cliff, they saw an Italian brigade watching the path and relaxing around a campfire.

The partisans readied themselves for martyrdom. They were moving swiftly, but the dry leaves they continuously stepped on precluded their intentions of moving quietly. "Please, move quietly," Hailu, whispered. All of the partisans had their grenades in their hands, ready to carry out the offensive.

"Please make it easy."

Suddenly, the Italians put out their campfires, signaling their awareness. "They must have heard our footsteps," said Hailu as they entered the riverbed.

The partisans readied themselves as they approached the Italians, waiting for Hailu's signal to unleash the attack.

One Italian soldier from the brigade designated with the responsibility of watching the other end of the pass heard a gunshot on the other side of the contingent. He opened fire in that direction, falsely thinking that the discernible gunshot indicated the partisan force's location. The other Italian soldiers followed suit.

"The soldier who fired that shot must be a new recruit for the Italians. A trained soldier would never do that," Hailu told his friends as they were passing the encirclement.

"Hailu!" shouted someone near him amidst the blazing bullets.

"Who are you?" asked Hailu.

"Kefelew," the man replied.

"People meeting in a night are so suspicious of each other! Where are the luggage and their carriers?" Hailu asked.

"I left them behind. Didn't I promise you that I would be on your side when you cross the river?"

Hailu felt tired.

"This must be the work of General Abebe. He must have sabotaged us," said Kefelew.

Hailu did not respond.

Kefelew's army safely reached Afkera, successfully circumventing the Italians. It was at this time that General Abebe's messenger reached them in Afkera. General Abebe wrote a letter to Kefelew. The letter delineated why the cease-fire was necessary.

"Why then did the Italians encircle our army," Kefelew asked the messenger.

"It was a mistake. We gave the name of the members of the Ancient Ethiopia's Heroes Association to the Italians to facilitate the handover. Since Kefelew did not sign the document, his name was left out. The Italians used this excuse to launch an offensive over your army."

An intense discussion ensued amongst the partisans in earnest about the relevance of Ancient Ethiopia's Heroes Association for the partisan force under Kefelew. About half of the partisans, dismissed the Association as irrelevant. The other half, including Hailu, supported membership of the Association and argued the need to establish a branch office of the Association in every region in Menz, Tegulet and Yifat.

"If we agree to join the Association, then what would be required from us for the establishment of the branch office of the Association?" a partisan asked.

"We need the rules and regulations of the Association," said Hailu.

"Please call the messenger," Kefelew ordered his aide. The messenger entered the room.

"We have decided to have a branch office of the Association here. We have also agreed to promote its cause. We need to have a copy of the rules and regulations of the Association"

"This can only be decided by the executive committee of the Association. I advise you to write a letter to General Abebe, stating your request," advised the messenger answering to Kefelew.

On the morrow, a letter addressed to General Abebe and copied to all the commanders was written by Kefelew asking to be allowed to join the Association. Later that day, Hailu's childhood friend and compatriot Tekle arrived in Afkera. "What a coincidence,"

Hailu said, while embracing his friend. "How is Addis Ababa?"

"Addis Ababa is in frantic preparation. The fascist Italians are mobilizing armies for their upcoming war against the British."

"We have heard the news."

"Good. The day before yesterday, when I was leaving Addis Ababa, I heard the news that an Italian general is expected to arrive in Addis Ababa. He is said to be Mussolini's messenger."

"What could the message be about?" Hailu inquired.

"I don't know. The compromise reached between the Italian government in Addis Ababa and General Abebe has created a serious political rift with Rome. Mussolini may have sent his messenger to give an ultimate decision on the matter; or his messenger may simply be in Addis Ababa to observe the political environment."

Hailu recalled the opposition to General Abebe on the same issue and was impressed by the division within Italy's political elite.

"When do you plan to leave for Addis Ababa?" Hailu asked after a long silence.

"First I will pass by Bulga. Then I will go to Addis Ababa. I will leave here tomorrow. I don't want to stay here too long."

"If you are passing through Bulga, then you will carry a letter written by Kefelew to General Abebc."

The letter was dispatched with Tekle. But after two weeks, Tekle returned with a letter from General Abebe. In the letter, it was stated that the rules and regulations of the Association could only be handed to a commander of a partisan unit in person.

General Abebe stated that the rules and regulations could only be given to Kefelew or another commander, but it could not be delivered through a messenger.

Hailu was chosen to go to Bulga and pick up the document.

Hailu started the journey to Bulga accompanied by his brother, ten soldiers, and Tekle.

Hailu was happy to have the opportunity to spend some time with his childhood friend Tekle. After traveling for half a day, Hailu's interest to know about his first wife Tiruwork was aroused.

"Well now, let me ask you a question," Hailu said. "Where does Tiruwork currently dwell?" Hailu inquired about his former wife, whom he had married in Addis Ababa without the consent of his father.

"She has married a good man, and she is a mother of two brave boys."

The news was discouraging, but Hailu could not help from asking more about her. "Where does she live?" he asked.

"In the Arsi province," Tekle answered.

Eventually, they reached the Adabai River, experiencing a wave of nostalgia. "Do you remember when we first attempted to flee to Addis Ababa we were too afraid to cross the Adabai River, so we returned to our village and consulted the village wizard?," Tekle laughed.

After an exhausting weeklong journey, they finally reached Bulga. Hailu was able to meet General Abebe after two days stay at the camp. The General told him about the agreement that had been reached with the Italians. Hailu felt that the reason the General was entering into a discussion with a regular soldier must be because he wished to assign him for a secret duty, something the General bestowed only for those who had his confidence.

"The Italians have changed their mind. Our secret service has informed us that a high official in Rome has arrived in Addis Ababa, and that Mussolini has directed him to defeat the Ethiopian armies in the rural areas before Italy goes to war with the British. As a result, the cease-fire has been canceled. In order to buy time to prepare for the final assault, the Italians have assigned General Nazi to meet us tomorrow morning. We have to kill him. He is responsible for organizing assassins who have killed many patriotic leaders"

Hailu waited for his instructions.

"I am happy that you came. You are a trained soldier and a sharpshooter. Your assignment is to shoot and kill General Nazi the moment he shakes my hand. Moreover, if the circumstances do not avail themselves for a sharp shot at the Italian General, you are authorized to shoot us both."

Hailu was shocked. "Why sir?" he asked. The order he received from General Abebe struck him like a punch in the stomach.

"It will be a great diplomatic victory for us if we are able to kill General Nazi, Governor of Shewa. I am replaceable. It will facilitate the ousting of the Italian occupiers."

Hailu stood still not knowing what to say. The General looked at him and said '' you are dismissed."

Hailu saluted and left with a heavy heart. He entered his assigned hut and lay down, instantly falling asleep. Hailu soon found himself trapped in a peculiar, but frightening dream, a dream that seemed so real. General Nazi entered the room, walking towards General Abebe with his hand extended smiling cordially at the Commander, unaware that his life was in the hands of an assassin. Hailu, undetected in the adjacent room, aimed his rifle. General Nazi and General Abebe shook hands and greeted each other warmly. At that moment, Hailu fired his weapon. However, the bullet did not penetrate General Nazi. Somehow, the bullet just bounced off General Nazi's chest as if he was bulletproof. Then, General Nazi looked right at Hailu, his gaze sadistically piercing Hailu's eyes. The General laughed, mocking Hailu's attempt to kill an immortal man. He stood beside General Abebe, daring Hailu to shoot. Hailu was bewildered; he had no idea what to do. Time froze. Hailu abruptly woke up in a cold sweat.

"What a dream. It was nonsense," he told his friend Tekle.

"Like what?" Tekle said, trying to wake up.

"I shot General Nazi, but he was bulletproof."

"How did you dream about him if you have never seen him? What did he look like in your dream?" Tekle joked.

Hailu smiled. "You are witty. I guess it is funny. But still I have dreamt about him."

"Go back to sleep. You have a long day tomorrow," Tekle said.

They slept. When Hailu woke up, he left for his assigned place to wait for the arrival of General Nazi.

General Nazi did not appear on the day of the scheduled appointment. Rather hundreds of thousands of Italian troops arrived and two warplanes flew over their heads. The planes distributed pamphlets that promised amnesty to those who handed themselves in to the Italians and complete annihilation to those who did not.

"Hailu, have you heard that some people had been defecting to the Italians after the cease-fire was reached?" Tekle asked.

"That is possible and it has always been like that. Many who vacillate betray during such times."

Wolde appeared. "Have you heard anything about the defection of some people and defected to the Italians?" he said.

"Who are the prisoners that defected?" Hailu asked.

"The first secretaries of the Association and his followers have defected. There was a division among the leaders about the necessity of entering into cease-fire agreement with the Italians. Because of this they were imprisoned."

The next day, the first encounter with the forward ground troops of the Italians and the partisans commenced. Army units moved out of the forest, each of them wearing white shema as camouflage attire. The limestone field was a God-sent disguise. The Battle of Bekur, in March 16, 1940, in Asagrt commenced. Twenty-two airplanes in formation began to bomb the forest.

Hailu looked at General Abebe. He was standing underneath a tree, calm and in full control of his surroundings. With his right hand projected out of his khaki cloak, he set directions for the army units.

As the sunset, the airplanes flew away for good. Hailu heard only the shots from afar. At times, the heavy artillery fire from the Italians swallowed up the sounds of the rifle and machinegun fire from the Ethiopian army. The vanguard fighters of the partisans eventually stopped the Italian army movement.

After the Italian planes had left, General Abebe disseminated orders to his people to stay organized in their units and move south. He sent a message to the front commanders to retreat to their camps, make a large campfire, leave it to burn, and then retreat, and meet him down south. Hailu and his friends joined the personal guards of General Abebe.

General Abebe had decided to save his army for the final battle, which was imminent after Italy had entered the Second World War on the side of the Axis powers.

Hailu walked beside General Abebe who was sitting on a mule. They descended a hill and a small river appeared. The movement of the partisan army stopped. "What is happening? Why don't they move forward?" General Abebe asked. Hailu looked down the river and saw some people signaling to him. He understood.

"Sir, let the soldiers drink from the river. Let's move forward and leave them behind," Hailu said. Then he led the mule past the soldiers and crossed the river.

"What did those soldiers say to you?" General Abebe inquired. "Did I forbid people to drink water?"

"Sir, you have bestowed many of them with traditional governorship title which requires decency and candor. They thought it would be shameful to drink water from a river with their bare hands in front of you."

General Abebe stood on high ground and looked back at the river. He saw every soldier's face buried in the water, drinking ferociously.

"I am considering giving you the traditional title," General Abebe said to Hailu.

"I am grateful. But I want it to be done after the ousting of the Italians."

"Some other day we will appoint Kefelew and you together."

The sun set in the west. The day was long and tiresome. Hailu slept.

Hailu was startled by an alarm that sounded during the middle of the night. He arose and headed towards his men. Italian assassins had overcome the bodyguards of General Abebe's family. Hailu tried to protect General Abebe's wife, however he was overwhelmed. He tried to stop the assassins. "Friends, let us shoot our rifles in continuity so that they seem like machinegun fire. This will halt the enemy," he ordered his men.

"It has worked. They have halted. Go on. One, two, three, yes, go on one, two, and three..." Hailu shouted.

The Italian assassins began to reassemble. Hailu saw another partisan group attacking the assassins. They were Balcha and his men.

An elite Italian unit was aiming to kill or take General Abebe prisoner. The offensive seemed to be an extension of the mercenary warfare the Italians had adopted earlier.

The assassins retreated haphazardly.

5

No one slept the rest of the night. Before the sunrise, Hailu heard from General Abebe's tent a cry of lament and he hurried there. "What happened?" he asked the first man he met.

"General Wondemneh Gebrekidan was killed."

Hailu wept for the famous patriot and when he had managed to compose himself, inquired how it had happened

"He was not aware that the Italians had broken the treaty. In the meantime, the Italians were bribing his field commanders. Yesterday morning when he woke up, he found himself deserted by his friends."

Hailu felt very sad.

"He went out and he was encircled. He fired his rifle and killed many. Then he put his rifle over his head and asked them to come and disarm him. Five mercenaries ran to him to be the first to take his hand and show their valor to the Italians. He disarmed the first mercenary and then killed them all. Captured after wounded, the Italians severed his right hand and his head and took them to the town Debre Birhan town."

"Those barbarians," Hailu exclaimed.

"Yes, they are beasts. In Debre Birhan, they displayed his head and made it face an Italian flag. They then made his right hand salute their flag!"

"We will avenge this," Hailu exclaimed.

Fascist Italy's last trial to make an alliance with the Ethiopian armies or to defeat them before facing the British failed miserably. The Ethiopian patriotic army emerged stronger than ever.

The Shewa army led by General Abebe has succeeded in avoiding annihilation with chemical and flamethrowers with minimal causalities. General Abebe received letters from the Generals in Gojjam and Kaffa. They wrote that they had avoided the Italian onslaught to prepare themselves for the final battle to crush the enemy. The Kaffa patriots wrote that they had already liberated Bonga.

Italy, in desperation, left about 30,000 Italian soldiers with hundreds of thousands of native soldiers. It transferred more than 300,000 Italian soldiers to the south and southwest to attack the British in Kenya and British Somaliland. This was the final preparation by fascist Italy to annihilate the Allied forces in the East African war theatre and then move on to North Africa.

6

Hailu and Wolde started their return journey to Menz with a copy of the Article of Association of the Ancient Ethiopia's Heroes Association. "Wolde what are you doing?" Hailu asked, puzzled. Wolde was putting his long traditional scarf around his waist and over it his trousers and belt.

"Don't you see my trousers are falling down because I have grown thin?"

"That is a problem for all of us. Anyway that is a great idea!" said Hailu and followed Wolde's example.

Hailu and Tekle separated near Debre Birhan. Tekle continued his way to Addis Ababa and the rest of them followed Hailu to Menz.

"Today is the third month since we left our village on an errand for General Abebe," commented Wolde.

Hailu felt fear and a longing for knowledge of the unknown things that might have happened in their home base. "Yes. We have not heard anything about our friends for the last three months," he said.

"I pray that nothing bad happened to our relatives and friends while we were away."

"Where did Meseret move to when we were encircled in Quatch? Have you heard anything?"

"I was only told that she was retreating to the west."

"Do you think that there may have been battles with our friends like we saw in Bulga?" Hailu consulted his brother.

"Let's hope for the best."

"How I long for my village!"

"Yes, longing grows more as one nears the longed place, so it is said by the fathers."

When they reached the top of the cliff above the village, they felt horrified. All the mansions were covered with soot. There seemed to be no one in them. It appeared to them as they ran down the cliff.

"What happened?" Hailu inquired when he met a soldier who came and received them.

The soldier kept quiet, avoiding telling them the sad news that happened during their absence.

"Was there a battle here also?" inquired Hailu.

"Yes and cruelty... Human cruelty overflowed the streams of Adabai."

"Where is Kefelew?"

"He has left with the partisans to a hiding place."

"Tell me who died amongst my relatives."

"You will hear it in the morning."

"No. This is wartime. I will not cry."

He mentioned ten names.

Hailu sat to mourn his deceased relatives. People came to comfort him. They also told him that the Italians were closing many of their camps. Hailu understood the Italian's motive. They were transferring their army to the border areas to face the British army.

"Where is Kefelew?" Hailu asked.

"He is in the cave. We kept it a secret since he has been ill for the last month."

"What was the diagnosis?"

"It was identified to be cholera."

"I want to talk to him."

"If you are not afraid of the plague you can talk to him."

Hailu saw Kefelew lying on a bed before him.

Hailu greeted the man who had come to be like a brother to him.

"Well you see this is how I am," said Kefelew, referring to the fact that he was ill and bedridden.

"Yes, but we should not lose the opportunity. I want my soldiers transferred to me and more than that, I want every commander to contribute fifty people to my group. I want to try to regain our lost territories." Hailu was determined.

"Will it be possible?"

"Yes. The Italians have given a great blow to our struggle before they went to the front to meet the British; but they have not destroyed us. Moreover, these last few days, they have closed many of their camps. So the conditions are now favorable."

"You may try, Hailu. I will need some time to recuperate," Kefelew said.

"Shall we wait until you are well to form the branch of the Ancient Ethiopian Heroes Association?"

"No, you must start it today. Also establish the branch of the postal service of the Association."

"Thank you."

"Why don't you tell me about the battle you were in?"

Hailu told him everything.

"How was General Abebe the moment you left him?"

"He was reassembling his soldiers to move to the highlands."

"Thank God," said Kefelew and drowsed off.

In the ensuing days, Hailu regained much of the lost territories and returned with his soldiers to Quatch.

7

It was in Quatch that Hailu had a very peculiar dream. In the morning, he told his friend Tadesse about it.

"What was it like?" Tadesse asked.

"Do you remember that beautiful horse that belonged to the grandfather of Fanaye and Meseret?"

"Yes."

"In my dream, you were seated on that white horse, and you were carrying their grandfather's spear and shield. You were riding fast. When you reached the wheat fields, you dropped the spear and gasha. I picked them up and called for you. But, I could not see you anywhere. I woke up thinking I was still holding the spear and gasha."

"You have dreamed a beautiful dream. If your dream comes true, you will have offspring from the descendants of the man. The meaning of the spear and gasha is sons and daughters. But I will have no offspring," Tadesse lamented.

"To sit on a white horse is a good omen. You were sitting on a white horse in my dream," Hailu protested.

"No Hailu. You only saw me riding the horse but in the end I disappeared," Tadesse looked at the earth. He believed in omens and dreams.

"This is simply a false dream. Anyway, Fanaye's grandfather has no daughters. I will not have offspring from his daughters nor will you die," said Hailu trying to change the topic of discussion.

"You could marry Fanaye's niece Meseret," Tadesse suggested.

"She is Sergeant Samuel widow. I have no such intentions," Said Hailu "Tadesse, why do you think our nights are filled with dreams?" asked Hailu.

"Yes, since we started our partisan life, our nights are filled with good and bad dreams."

"These days we dream much. I think it may be for the reasons that we see much, do much, and pass through life and death continuously. By the way, have you heard about Meseret? Don't forget she is the widow of Sergeant Samuel."

"Yes. She survived the onslaught. She is currently residing in Yekese. She left the day before the last wipeout campaign reached here." Answered Tadesse

Hailu kept quiet.

Part Nine: War, Love, and Responsibility
Meseret

1

Meseret and Mahlet started their return journey from Yekese to Nib Washa. When they reached the edge of the escarpment, Meseret looked at Adabai River in the gorge and turning her face, she scanned the endless prairie that stretched to Sasit. It seemed ages passed as scenes flashed through her mind. She remembered her uncle Samson, Mahlet's father, traveling to the north with his fifty followers without any one of them returning from the Northern War fronts. The scene changed to her journey with Mahlet to Sasit to become patriots. She smiled as she remembered her marriage to Sergeant Samuel. It all overwhelmed her. She broke down in tears. Mahlet understood why she was crying. She also cried remembering their short yet seemingly long adventures. Her soldiers also remembered Sergeant Samuel and they too cried silently. Nib Washa was only a short way down the escarpment. They cleared their eyes, went down, and entered their grandmother's home. The family received them with joyous tears. They had not seen Meseret and Mahlet in two years since the demise of Sergeant Samuel.

Nib Washa, apart from the burned-out houses, which Meseret had witnessed two years earlier, had not changed much, except the fact that people had grown poor and the church in Jer had grown older. The elite Kahn Yohannes has grown very thin and old but he was still performing his sacred duties.

Every day Meseret would stand on the edge of the prairie, fathoms its horizon, and then turn her face to look down at Adabai River in the magnificence gorge. Every Sunday she would go to church. She wondered why prayers remain unanswered. After the ceremony, one Sunday Meseret went and sat beside the priest. He knew that she must have something to ask him. He waited for her. "Does God hear our prayers?" she asked him.

"Yes, he hears and yes, he speaks" he said to her. She felt from his voice the gravity of his answer.

"How?" she asked him.

"The Ark of the Covenant is a communication tent. God spoke through the Ark of the Covenant to Moses. The Ark of the Covenant spoke to Emperor Eyasu I, three hundred years ago. The guardians should have prayed. The European war has started and Italy will fall. If Britain or Russia overplay their role and try to subjugate this land, God will avenge them. Be strong in your prayers. Be God's instrument."

She wanted to believe him. She cried in happiness.

He also seemed happy to share his knowledge. "Be strong. Marry one of the patriot leaders. Guide them and give them strength. You are God's instrument." He added. "These trying times will pass. God tests His people, but He will not forsake them."

The next Sunday, during the sermon in the church, Kahn Yohannes dwelt on the issue in detail. Meseret felt it was mainly directed at her. Nevertheless, everyone was touched and blessed. The Kahn elucidated the matter as follows:

"The European war has started. Our mother Mary of Zion has heard our wailing. God is to end these trying times. Cleanse your soul. If you pray and cleanse your soul and accept his mercy and emerge humble, free of human weakness, and full of forgiving, these trying times will be rewarding and will bring you closer to God. If these trying times create greed, hatred, vengeance and self-grandeur, then you will be lowly people like the fascists, which you have been fighting with God's help.

Believe in your God's mercy and his greatness. He will deliver you from the fascists. If the British, Russians and the Americans other than helping you, try to extend the trying times, your God will punish them. God will deliver you.

Let us pray. Our Father, who art in Heaven. Hallowed be thy name, thy Kingdom come..."

When Meseret and Mahlet went out of the church, they met Tadesse and Fanaye praying at the outer walls of the church.

Meseret was calm and accepted Tadesse and Fanaye in grace. "How do you do Fana? Let us exchange kisses again. It's been a long time since we've last seen each other," Meseret tried to feign that she was happy to see them.

"Meseret you have lost too much weight," said Fana seeing Meseret very pale. Everybody had lost weight in these trying times, but Fana thought that Meseret looked particularly unhealthy. "You have grown very pale. Oh, I am going to cry," Fana, said.

A machinegun fire was heard. Tadesse along with his men and Meseret's soldiers left for the direction where continuous gunfire came from. Meseret and Fanaye remained and continued the conversation.

"How is life here?" Meseret asked Fanaye.

"It is fine, especially after we regained our lost territories," Fanaye replied. "We have expanded the territory under us. Haven't you heard that since the territory has expanded, Kefelew has made his base in Imweta?"

"Yes, I have heard that."

"Have you heard about Beshah?" Fanaye asked.

"I was expecting you to tell me about him since I heard Hailu came from General Abebe's camp in Bulga, you might have got information from him." Meseret said.

"Yes, he met him. He left Beshah in the Danakil desert. He said that General Abebe's led army was tactically retreating and Uncle Beshah was with his soldiers accompanying General Abebe." Fana informed Meseret.

"I like Beshah very much. He is an uncle, a teacher and a hero. He is a kind and grand person to me. If Samuel was alive I would have been with him." Meseret said remembering her times with Beshah in Sasit, then in General Abebe's camp.

"Hailu told me that he mentioned you to Uncle Beshah. He described you as a sister whom he cannot praise enough, 'She is just magnificent,' he had said."

"That is kind of him."

The two sisters shared stories and joked the whole day. The men at last came and announced their victory. Hailu greeted Meseret and sat at the opposite corner. Tadesse greeted Meseret and sat near Hailu. Dinner was served. They ate their dinner after the priest had given his blessings. The priest put down his rifle, washed his hands, and sat near Hailu.

After dinner, Meseret and Fanaye got up to go outside.

"Meseret, where are you going?" Tadesse asked.

"We just want to have a look outside," Fanaye answered, and they went out. It was Fanaye's idea that they go out and look at the country as they used to do when they were children. They looked down at Adabai and their hearts were filled with old memories. It brought tears to their eyes but they did not discuss any particular issue. Silently they returned home.

All of the guests stood up from their seats, honoring Meseret. "Please sit down," she said. Then she went to her seat and sat down, but she saw that the guests were still standing. She stood up and repeated her request more forcefully this time. "Please sit down." She felt troubled. She looked at Hailu, but he was looking at his feet coyly.

"We will not sit down until you agree to what we are begging you to do," Kahn Yohannes said.

Meseret suspected what they were planning. In wartime, nothing seems normal.

"Just agree," Mahlet said.

"Yes," said her soldiers.

The Kahn then spoke about marriage and the role of the institution in fulfilling human and divine purposes. Then he told her why they were standing. He remembered Sergeant Samuel and told her that he must live in her heart and in the hearts of all the people. He reminded her of her role and destiny. It was after a long sermon that he begged her to marry Hailu. He reminded her in passing that the marriage would give better protection for her and her child from the mercenary assassins. Her soldiers and Mahlet seemed to be happy.

Meseret sobbed. Everybody kept quiet. There was long, quiet passage of time. She clasped her hands and put them on her breasts. She then moved her head up and down to show her agreement. Mahlet remembered Meseret's similar response to Samuel's advice two years earlier during the occasion when the Italians threw out patriots from a flying airplane. At that time, she had also moved her head up and down in the same manner while tears flowed from her eyes, showing she had understood Samuel's advice.

Meseret and Hailu got married in the next week.

2

The following Sunday they got married, Meseret and Hailu went to a local church together to witness the sermon of the renowned Kahn Yohannes. People traveled from far away villages to listen to the sermon of the high priest. Meseret told Hailu about the priest while they were walking to the church. Then she asked him an unrelated question, "How was your army life in Addis Ababa?"

"It was not very rewarding," he replied. "Half the time, I spent guarding palaces, government granaries, offices, etc. while the other half, I spent cutting wood and carrying it from Addis Alem to Addis Ababa."

"Why?"

"There is a major shortage of wood needed for construction and fuel in Addis Ababa."

"Do the Italian soldiers perform the same duty for their government?" she asked him.

"No. They are only soldiers. They conduct war exercises even when they are off duty."

"How was your home life?"

"Home life?" he asked as if he has not heard it.

"You heard me."

"Usually after hazardous work, we sat below the sky to take our food. We took some cooked barley flour from our sheepskin bags, mixed it with water, and then ate it."

"Don't you have a home?" her questions were starting to agitate Hailu, but he continued to answer them.

"I used to have a home. But I usually did not spend much time in it."

"Soldiers' life must have been troublesome. Why didn't Samuel tell me about it?" Meseret asked.

"Samuel was a sergeant. He was not expected to carry wood or perform farm duties for the government officials. He must have told you about his professional life."

"Then it means there wasn't much difference between the life you lead here and the one you spent toiling. Maybe the present one is better," Meseret said.

"It is not better."

"Why?"

"Here you live amidst misery. The Italians burnt the grain many times and drove the cattle from the farmers, and we are forced to take counter-measures by expropriating the cattle and burning the fields of the peasants who were loyal to the Italians. Things go on and on, violence begets more violence. The peasants get famished. They die of hunger, epidemic diseases and other related ailments."

"Yes that is true," said Meseret wiping the tears that came to her eyes. "Our peasants were poor people even before the war. Currently they pay taxes in two directions. We punish them for being loyal to the Italians and so do the Italians for being loyal to their country and us. War is a disaster!"

"I remember what happened two years ago. The Italians overran the loyal region, expropriating the region's cattle and grain. As a result, a famine commenced. We had no alternative but to take punitive measures against areas controlled by the Italians. We brought cattle and grain and distributed them to our people. We even slaughtered the ox of a notorious traitor and gave the food to the villagers. They ate it but became sick because the meat was bad. Even I contracted the epidemic and was taken ill."

"Oh God," she exclaimed.

"Then I was taken into a cave, and I was left with my rifle. Kebede would come by every day to give me food and water. One day, I heard a war cry and in frenzy, I thought the Italians were coming."

Meseret stifled a smile.

"Why did you smile," Hailu asked

"Sorry, I think what we have been doing is amazing. I mean what Ethiopia has been able to accomplish so far against the Italians. We have started a struggle in a most miserable situation. The Italians have the airplanes, the tanks, the artillery, the money and the grain. They can rain poisonous liquids on us and may even intentionally spread diseases to kill us.

Both of them kept quiet and immersed in old memories entered the church and kissed the walls.

.

Mussolini's nightmare

Part Ten: The Tides Change
Hailu/Meseret

1

Kefelew invited Meseret and Hailu to Imweta for a luncheon party in their honor. Hundreds of guests attended the luncheon. After lunch, the floor opened for traditional dancing.

Meseret discovered that Hailu was an accomplished dancer and was happy about his performance. "Here, take my scarf. Go on dancing," she said putting the scarf on his shoulder. He put the scarf around his waist and began dancing with a rhythmic shake of his shoulders like leaves swinging in the wind.

"Great Hailu!" people were joyously shouting and clapping their hands in step with the song. Another partisan was singing.

Meseret laughed enwrapped in happiness.

The dancing stopped when reports came of an expected attack from Italian forces at Molale Camp. One of the Italian commanders in Molale camp, Lieutenant Giovanni heard about the ceremony that was taking place in Imweta, which was near Molale, and took upon himself to try to capture the partisan leaders as they assembled for the celebration.

Kefelew and his army perceived the move as reckless.

"I will take the right wing and you can take the left wing, we will encircle them," Hailu suggested to Kefelew.

"You chose the difficult side. Well, it's ok," said Kefelew. "Let the rest of you continue with the celebration. Hailu and I will be enough to counter the barbarians," Kefelew said to the other commanders invited for the occasion.

"I have heard that the commander of the Italians in Molale is a young adventurous lieutenant," Hailu said to Kefelew while they were on their pursuit. "This must be his plan."

"Yes, it must be. He seemed not to care about danger. He must be an inexperienced soldier. Good luck," Kefelew said.

It was a simple operation. The Italian army assailed in two directions, and its commander was taken prisoner with five mercenaries. The rest of the Italian soldiers retreated to Molale.

Amidst the festival, a general assembly gave judgment to lieutenant Giovanni and his fellow native mercenary prisoners.

"The native mercenaries, since they have betrayed their country, deserve the death penalty. However, the Italian, in accordance to the regulation of the Ancient Ethiopia's Patriotic Association, and the Red Cross laws, should be considered a war prisoner," a partisan recommended.

"I don't agree with what my fellow friend suggested about the punishment for the local traitors that fought against us," Hailu snapped. "If we remember our tradition, during the lifetime of our late commander Gizachew Haile, we should convince them to fight the Italians."

Eventually, the Italian war prisoner was handed over to Hailu. Hailu left with his men and the war prisoners, including Giovanni.

"Hailu, we should plan to capture the camp in Molale next week," confided Kefelew. "We might not need you for this operation. You have to monitor the movement of Italians at Sasit camp.

Hailu and Meseret returned to their home with Giovanni. In the morning, Meseret observed Giovanni. His hair was red and his body looked like unbaked dough. His eyes were blue, but they seemed blank, as if he were blind.

"Are you hungry?" she asked him in Amharic. After a pause and a bewildered look from Giovanni, she asked him, "You don't know our language. Ah?" However, Giovanni still did not understand. He gently shook his head from one side to the other, sitting on the earth seat with a confounded countenance.

"Ham, ham," she said, while moving, gesticulating as if she were eating something. Now he understood, he nodded and said, "Yes," the only word he knew in Amharic.

Meseret brought him the Ethiopian bread (injera) with peppered sauce (wot). He tried to eat it, but he could not. Meseret felt sorry for him. She went out to the villages and brought back some eggs. She had heard somewhere that the Italians liked eggs. He ate the cooked eggs with delight and smiled.

"Good boy," she said in Amharic, patronizing the Italian without knowing it.

Meseret went to find Mahlet as she had acquired some basic Italian words during her captivity. Mahlet was able to greet Giovanni in his own language, and in time, the two of them developed a simple, but meaningful rapport.

2

Giovanni spent his prison time under house arrest. However, for obvious reasons, Giovanni was hoping that the Italians would soon rescue him from his capturers, as unlikely as that was.

In the traditional house arrest, the prisoner is confined to a village and he could move freely in the village and interact with the villagers. Giovanni liked to spend much time with Mahlet. There was a language barrier between them, yet they seemed to understand each other. Sometimes, they seem to share jokes, laughing for reasons not clear to others. Meseret was also curious how the two communicated. She asked Mahlet but she did not get a satisfactory answer.

Hailu had observed that Giovanni tried to romance with Mahlet. Hailu thought that it would be better to find him another woman to marry him. He decided that if he told Giovanni about this plan, he would stop his efforts to seduce Mahlet, which is Meseret's sister, and from the gentry.

"Well Giovanni" said Hailu one day, in an attempt to speak to him through an interpreter. "We will marry you to a beautiful lady when we regain our independence, after first christening you."

"I will marry only Mahlet."

"Mahlet will not marry a non-Christian."

"I am Christian," he answered.

"A Christian?" Hailu was puzzled.

"Yes, a Catholic as such."

"Ah, yes but still you are not a Christian," said Hailu.

"Let our wish come true. Who knows our destiny?" Giovanni sighed.

"Yes, all is in the hands of God."

It was not long after that Mahlet told Meseret about her fondness of Giovanni. Meseret laughed, taking it as a joke, but after observing the seriousness of Mahlet's face, calmed down and asked her if she was making a well-thought-out decision.

"I love only Giovanni..."

"It is ok," said Meseret and they sat under a tree looking at the sun setting behind the mountain. "The human heart," Askale mused.

3

A week after they returned from Imweta news came to Hailu that Kefelew has captured Molale town from the Italians. He also received a letter from his friend Ahmed sent from Harar. In his letter, Ahmed informed Hailu that he had come from Jimma to Harar three months earlier. He wrote about the commencement of the war in Europe. Hailu was exhilarated when another letter reached him from the Ancient Ethiopia's Heroes Association, enumerating the next tasks in the struggle against fascism. It encouraged all members to oust the Italians from the towns.

Hailu told Meseret the contents of the letters and discussed with her a plan to expand their territories by ousting the Italians from Sasit town and Tegulet.

"That is the territory that belongs to my uncle, Commander Beshah." Meseret said firmly.

"We could hand it over to him when he comes back from Bulga." Hailu suggested. Meseret agreed. Commander Beshah had retreated a year earlier with his army to his friend General Abebe, after the surrender of General Kebede to the Italians after the fall of Sela Dingay.

"Commander Beshah's army, along General Abebe's army might be pushing their territory towards Addis Ababa," added Hailu when he saw indecision on her face.

"Oh, how long will it be before I see him again?" Meseret murmured. She agreed that their army should press forward towards Tegulet.

During the following days, the partisans all over the country became more hopeful. Hailu became confident of victory. He began to walk around assuredly. Rumors of Italy's defeat abounded.

"Have you heard that the Italian camp at Woreyilu has been taken over and the commander has been killed?" a rumormonger may ask.

"No, I haven't. I will send somebody and verify the news," Hailu would answer.

"I heard that the Italian General in Debre Birhan was assassinated," would say another rumormonger.

"That's very good news," Hailu might respond.

Hailu and his friends were confident that Italians were losing. Kefelew had captured the town of Molale from the Italians recently.

This was the main topic of discussion during the feast of Archangel Gabriel, which Hailu and Meseret hosted. Partisans, including Kefelew and Tessema Irgete, came from faraway places just to share with each other the good news. Kefelew received a warm welcome when he came to the feast for capturing Molale from the Italians. It was a time in which partisans would confer together and circulate the good news among one another. "God is smiling down on us," one partisan commented.

For the commanders assembled in Hailu's house for drinking, eating and dancing, it was a jubilant moment. Soldiers and commanders overflowed the huts of the village to celebrate the occasion; some were even dancing with beers in their hands.

"Hey! Ho! Look!" said a partisan pointing at the mountain in the north.

"Look at what?" one partisan non-chalantly asked. Then he turned his face in that direction. "Oh God!" he gasped.

"Let's go and inform the commander!"

"Hailu, how could you? You were intending to betray us?" said Kefelew, while Tesema listened.

"Will you please hear me out?" Hailu exclaimed. "In the name of the Archangel Gabriel, that was not my intention. I have stationed scouts all around. I don't know how they passed them," Hailu pleaded.

"Anyway thanks. Let's depart in the direction of Mofer Wouha," Kefelew said with sarcasm.

"I know that Hailu has taken all the necessary precautions. You cannot be angry with him." Meseret retorted.

Hailu assembled his men and went with his scouts and his soldiers to repulse the enemy. He knew the Italian offensive was weak, only trying to display its presence.

Kefelew, the other partisan leaders, and their constituents entered the river. "We will have to punish Hailu for his treacherous transgression," Kefelew bristled.

Hailu and his men climbed the valley; and at last, he stationed his soldiers near a narrow path that concealed their presence from the Italians.

"The Italians don't seem to be aware of our presence here. They have only observed Kefelew and the others going away. They seem in a hurry to reach the river," Wolde observed.

"I hope so. If they come near this cliff, they will not pass it," Hailu said and then saw the first batch of Italian soldiers approaching. He fired his machinegun. Those Italians who were unprepared for battle suffered heavy causalities, but continued the fight. The battle reached a stalemate.

"Wondimu, Come back, if possible kill a few traitors, and come back," a soldier of Hailu has called out to the enemy's side.

"Shut up! What are you doing?" said Hailu. "You are calling a name of a friend of ours, which is senseless."

"Hailu look! Kefelew and the others are returning back to your home," said a friend of his. Once they saw Hailu engaged in battle with the Italians, Kefelew and the other commanders returned to Hailu's home to continue the festival.

Hailu climbed a tree and saw that the Italians were retreating to Sasit. "They are retreating," Hailu, informed them.

They went up the cliff and they saw Wondmu and some of their friends killed. "What is it?" Hailu mused.

"What was Wondimu doing with the Italians? Did they capture and kill him?" asked Hailu.

"He was bought by the Italians. I was suspicious about Wondmu. Yesterday they left to an unknown destiny. I thought they must have betrayed us. That was the reason why I called his name and told him to kill them and come back as was planned. The Italians must have believed me and shot him with his friends," said the soldier who previously called out to Wondmu during the battle, giving him directions without authorization.

"I understand," said Hailu. When the Italian commander was informed about the message to Wondmu, he believed that they were led into a trap."

"Yes, he must have believed your bluff, and they machinegunned him. So much for the life of a traitor," said Hailu.

Sheferaw Irgete, one of the commanders who were attending the feast came with his soldiers to Hailu. "We met your scouts down the river. They told us the full story. That is why Kefelew returned to your home, and I came here to help you," Sheferaw explained.

During the feast, detailed plans were drawn to oust the Italians from Sasit and Sela Dingay. It was not long after those native mercenaries started to betray the Italians and joined the partisans. Meseret facilitated the change of alliance by writing to the native mercenaries to change sides at this point where the enemy was losing the war.

The next day, a man called Debotch, a native mercenary leader in the Sasit Italian camp switched sides, along with his soldiers and surrendered to Meseret.

Meseret was happy when she saw Debotch and his men. She knew why they came; they must have heeded her advice. "How are you Debotch? Welcome," Meseret said and greeted him warmly. "Did you receive my letter? Yes you did. I heard you are a brave fighter. We are proud that you have come to us."

"Well, I also came with my friends."

Food and beer was served around the campfire that was hastily organized, they began to talk. Debotch told them about the Italian camp, its manpower and strength.

"Nobody is to mistreat them. These are my strict instructions," whispered Meseret to the soldiers who were looking at these men with contempt.

"Meseret, we are going to drive the Italians out of Tegulet by tomorrow," said Hailu inviting Meseret to share her views on the issue.

"Do not forget that Tegulet is my uncle Beshah's territory," Meseret reminded Hailu firmly. It was Beshah with his camp in Sasit who was responsible for Tegulet before he was ousted by the Italians and he was forced to retreat to General Abebe administered territory.

"I know that. We want to drive the Italians out and then hand it over to Commander Beshah later on. In light of the letter from the Ancient Ethiopia's Patriots Association, I think this will be the right decision."

The battle that took place the next day was relatively minor. The Italians and the Bandas were low in morale, and they retreated. The territory of Tegulet was freed from Italian occupation within a week. Meseret remembered not only Commander Beshah, but also her late husband Samuel. Beshah had been stationed in Sasit when Meseret and Mahlet joined the Ethiopian battalion four years ago. Sasit fell in a single day's fight. The strategic town of Sela Dingay was captured from the Italians in a half-day's battle. Three years earlier, it had taken the Italians nearly two years to snatch Sela Dingay from the Ethiopian army.

4

Meseret remained in Sasit after writing a letter to her uncle Beshah about their intention to hand over the administration of Tegulet once he returned with his soldiers to the region. The letter explained why the measure to liberate Tegulet was taken without consulting him.

The third day after the letter to Commander Beshah had been sent, Kebede, one of her uncle's loyal soldiers came to Sasit. Kebede was the most loyal soldier, and never left Commander Beshah's side even for an hour. "Why are you not with my uncle Beshah?" Meseret asked Kebede upon seeing him.

"I do not know how to put it, but Commander Beshah has been taken, prisoner," he said and began to sob. Meseret joined him, crying as if she had received news of his death. People began to enter the room shocked.

"How was he taken prisoner?" Meseret asked.

"He heard that you had taken over Tegulet, and so he rushed over here to claim his governorship of Tegulet. But the Italians were waiting for him..."

"Lady Meseret, do not cry. He is not dead," many voices tried to comfort her but she knew that the Italians, in order to avenge the many Italians killed by him, would not spare him. They would not forget the bridges he destroyed on the road from Dessie to Addis Ababa. He was and had been the shining star of the patriotic war. She also knew about the harsh order from Mussolini to execute any captured Ethiopian.

Hailu entered the room, after a while left it with a broken heart, and stood outside. Meseret was crying saying that she was the cause of the death of her uncle.

"Where did they take him?" asked Meseret

"To the town of Debre Birhan," answered Kebede, informing her that a rescue mission would be impossible.

Not long afterward, Meseret heard that the Italians had hanged her uncle. Her kind, magnificent, brave, loving uncle had been martyred. She remembered the first moments she joined the army at Sasit commanded by Beshah. She remembered Samuel, her first husband who was with Commander Beshah's battalion. "Oh my uncle, if I forget you..." she cried. A day had never passed without her remembering him. His memory lived within her up to the end. Beshah would remain in her mind as youthful as the last time she saw him. Memory never grows old nor does a man die as long as he is remembered by his people.

Commander Beshah, Tesema and Gizachew were the three commanders who protected Yifat, Tegulet and Menz from the Italian onslaught in the first years of the attrition war.

Meseret accepted the guests who came to express their respect for Beshah. They mourned Beshah as befits a hero, in war songs and with salvos of machinegun fire. People from the surrounding areas gathered singing war songs while the women wailed. Poems about the exploits of Beshah and his followers were recited as rifles were being fired into the sky. The death and exploits of Samuel were also remembered.

The Kahn was also very sad about the death of Beshah. The priests conducted the religious rites that started during the night and continued into the morning. The Kahn spoke at last. He blessed the congregation in the name of the Father, the Son, and the Holy Ghost. He spoke about the future. He seemed to sense that the congregation had to be alert about the future.

"My children in spirit please keep in your heart what I am going to say. It will guide you in the coming years. Our victory with God's will is a reality. The liberation of towns in Tegulet in a one-day battle is evidence of the Fascist's inevitable defeat. After our liberation, the trials of the past five years should be the basis for cleansing your soul to live a life that will bring you nearer to the will of God; this could be done by choosing to lead a life more upright than the Fascists.

You should be humble before your God. You should be forgiving. In Matthew's Gospel it is written, "For if you forgive men their trespasses, your heavenly Father will forgive you; but if you do not forgive men their trespasses, then neither will your Father forgive yours."

"Prayer and hard work will help you improve your life and help you realize your dreams for technological advancement. It will enable you to have lasting peace. On the contrary, if you lead a life of gluttony, voracity, ravenousness, greed, insatiability and self-indulgence, God will bring more trying times. Remember Sodom and Gomorrah; they were destroyed for such sins. Tekle had told me about the towns and cities in Italy's control. They have become like Sodom and Gomorrah. When you enter these towns, do not be tempted. Let God save you from temptation. When you say the daily prayers remember what it says about temptation. Let us say the Lord's Prayer together."

"Our Father who art in Heaven, hallowed be thy name, thy kingdom come, thy will be done on earth as it is in heaven, give us this day our daily breads; and forgive our trespasses, as we forgive those who trespass against us, and lead us not into temptation, but deliver us from evil. Amen."

5

A letter from Tekle announced that the Italians had already lost the battle with the British. He wrote that during the start of the war between the Allies on the one hand and the

Axis powers, the Axis powers, which included Fascist Italy, were victorious. He wrote that the Italians were able to capture Hargessa in British Somaliland and Moyale in Kenya from the British. He went on to say that the British and the allies were growing powerful and, after a major assault the Italians were surrendering en masse. He advised the Ethiopian army everywhere to exert the utmost energy in creating havoc on the Italians.

He added that the diplomatic circles in Addis Ababa were predicting that the defeat of the Italians in Ethiopia would be a landmark as the first victory of the allies against the axis powers in what is known as the Second World War.

In the next week after the liberation of Sasit, the towns in Shewa fell in the hands of the patriots. General Abebe's Army occupied Debre Birhan and the towns on the way to Addis Ababa. Sela Dingay, Sasit, Molale were taken by the army under Kefelew.

A letter from General Abebe addressed to all patriotic forces explained that the Emperor would reach Addis Ababa in May. Everybody was excited by the news and the possibility to see the Emperor. Everybody in Shewa was invited to travel to Addis Ababa to meet with the Emperor.

No matter how eager Kefelew was to meet the Emperor in Addis Ababa, there was no way he could reach Addis Ababa without facing General Abebe Aregai. The General's order to return Tegegne Busera's machinegun had not been obeyed, nor had Kefelew shown himself before the Council headed by General Abebe, to answer charges and sign in person membership to Ancient Ethiopia's Heroes Association.

The Ethiopian army in Shewa, (with the exception of those led by Kefelew), led by General Abebe, moved to Addis Ababa, and was stationed outside the city. The British troops entered Addis Ababa while the Ethiopian Army, under General Abebe watched from the hilltop as ordered by the Emperor.

The British forces entered Addis Ababa on April 5. This was considered the first victory of the Allied forces over the Axis powers.

6

From his village in Gulele, Tekle went to the outskirts of Addis Ababa to give security briefings to General Abebe. He briefed him that the British and the allies considered the defeat of the Italians as the first victory of the allies against fascism.

General Abebe heard him attentively. Tekle continued. "The allies' war is currently concentrated in the North Africa war theatre. The defeat of the Italians in Ethiopia, in East Africa will open the way for the British and the allies to concentrate on the North African war."

"Will they honor Ethiopia's independence?"

"It seems that they had considered the Ethiopian patriotic army as guerrilla formations for hit and run warfare. Currently, they seem to understand that the Ethiopian army is not a guerrilla formation. This I think should be emphasized."

General Abebe Aregai dismissed him. Tekle, confident that he has made his point with General Abebe, traveled to Tegulet to visit Hailu and Meseret. He carried a message to Kefelew from the Emperor. He smiled foreseeing the numerous questions he would have to answer from the curious Meseret. He thought that Meseret would be impressed to hear that the victories East African campaign by the British consisted of almost all races that included Ethiopians, British, Sudanese, Kenyan, Rhodesian, South African, Indian, Nigerian, Ghanaian, and Free French Forces.

When he reached Menz, the Axis powers were advancing towards Cairo. The ally forces, led by the British, were in haste to finish the East African campaign and move to Cairo.

He gave Kefelew the Imperial order to join the British forces when they moved to Dessie and then to Ambalage, in the North. Three-fourths of the soldiers in Kefelew and the other armies joined the British. After three days stay, Tekle left for Addis Ababa. He has to coordinate security issues in Addis Ababa in preparation for the return of Emperor Haile Selassie to his capital city.

During the days of the Emperor's return to his capital city, Tekle was charged with the most important task of overseeing security matters within the patriots. His role in the current affairs of Ethiopia had skyrocketed. Tekle chose a strategic position below the Saint Mary Church on Entoto (Entoto Maryiam) waiting for the emergence of the Emperor from Fitche to the summit of Entoto Mountain. Suddenly machinegun fire broke out.

The Patriotic Ethiopian Army dispersed and took a position. Later it was discovered that the shots were fired by the British soldiers killing the camels, which transported logistics of the new Ethiopian battalion army led by General Wingate.

Emperor Haile Selassie emerged and the Kahns and clergies of the church of Saint Mary welcomed the Lion of Judah and the protector of the Ark of the Covenant with religious hymns and dances. The Ethiopian army, led by General Abebe welcomed the Emperor with a military parade. The Emperor entered the church surrounded by the clergy and the Ethiopian army Generals and officers. The Emperor participated in the church sermon.

The journey to Addis Ababa started with the South African motorized units and tank division. The motorized unit and tank division had defeated the Italians in Mogadishu, Harar, and along with the Ethiopian patriots, it moved to Dessie and forced the surrender of the Duke of Aosta in Gondar. This was followed by the Ethiopian Second Battalion led by General Wingate on a white horse. The army was composed of the Gojjam, Gondar, the Tigrai army, and the Imperial Bodyguard, known as the Black Lions who had lived in exile in Sudan and Kenya and joined the Emperor in Sudan. Then moved the imperial motorcade accompanied by the former Addis Ababa Equestrian Police. The Emperor sat with great dignity in an open vehicle.

Tekle watched the procession. The equestrian police division had been the one commanded by General Abebe before the Italian fascists' invasion. Its loyalty to General Abebe proved to be undisputable, even under the British administration. This gave comfort to Tekle.

The Ethiopian Army, who came from all provinces and led by General Abebe, followed the Emperor's motorcade.

Tekle watched. He was confident about the safety of the Emperor. The palace was just less than half way from the mountain and Menelik's palace. Addis Ababa's population was ecstatic. The citizens were thanking God by kissing the ground and with joyful tears.

Tekle could not restrain his tears. He watched the Black Lions here and there. He saw Ahmed and greeted him with a sign. Ahmed smiled back.

"Ethiopia has reinstated its Emperor and the British have defeated the Axis powers for the first time in the East African war theatre," thought Tekle.

The Emperor made a speech as soon as he reached his palace. The speech pierced the souls of the patriots and the loyal citizens.

"I thank the Almighty God for enabling me to stand amidst you. This is a day neither the archangels in heaven nor the military powers on earth could foresee ..."

He continued his speech and declared Ethiopia's independence. He thanked the British and declared that the enemies of Britain are the enemies of Ethiopia.

The next day, the patriotic Ethiopian army who came from the nearby provinces, led by General Abebe, staged an impressive military show. General Abebe was appointed Minster of War.

7

A week after the Emperor's return to his capital city an order came from the Emperor to Kefelew and his army ordering them to go to

Debre Birhan and wait for him. Another decree from the Emperor followed which demanded the handing over of any Italian prisoners in custody to the central government.

The news about the transfer of the prisoners to the central government was very disturbing to Mahlet and Giovanni. Meseret also found it very hard to comfort Mahlet as she was crying out her heart. Some even took it as disgraceful for an Ethiopian woman to be crying over an Italian man.

"Meseret, will you help me and Giovanni escape into the Adabai Gorge?" Mahlet pleaded.

"To what end. Do you want to be a shifta? Both of you will be killed."

"So what do you suggest?"

"Giovanni will be taken to Addis Ababa. At most, they would imprison him for some years; occasionally, we will go and visit him in Addis Ababa. When he finishes his sentence, you two will get married," Meseret said.

"What if they kill him?"

"I think the Emperor's people are like us. We did not kill him but kept him under house arrest. They may even pardon him."

Mahlet felt better.

At last, Hailu got ready to take Giovanni to Debre Birhan to hand him over to the authorities. With Meseret's insistence, Meseret and Mahlet joined the company of ten people selected to hand over the prisoners.

When Hailu escorted Giovanni into the truck, there were already many Italian prisoners inside. They were laughing and in jolly mood to have been transferred to the central Ethiopian government, which they were sure would transfer them to the British forces.

Giovanni was crying and was upset about his separation from Mahlet.

The scene of Giovanni's climb onto the truck remained embedded in Meseret's memory. Mahlet burst into tears, ran to the truck and held the door tightly, and continued sobbing. Giovanni again bursts out into tears. The soldiers with Hailu pulled Mahlet away from the truck.

The Italian prisoners near Giovanni pulled him down aggressively. They were disturbed by his actions. Some even punched him in the gut. The hardliner fascists, who believed in the fascist theory of racial separation, were discomforted.

Meseret was trying to console Mahlet when Hailu came towards them. "Hailu, you will take both of us to Addis Ababa in the future. I would like to visit Addis Ababa and Mahlet can visit Giovanni."

Hailu was still embarrassed by Mahlet's behavior. But to avoid confrontation with Meseret he smiled and said, "Yes of course. My plan is to take all my family to Addis Ababa once the war is over."

Mahlet felt hopeful. In the belief that there would be a reunion with Giovanni, Mahlet's tears stopped flowing. She leaned into the embrace of Meseret and fell into a deep sleep. Meseret slowly laid her on the ground, making a pillow for her head with her belongings.

8

Emperor Haile Selassie, with Minister of War, General Abebe and other dignitaries, came to Debre Birhan not long after his return to Addis Ababa. General Abebe left the decision for insubordination to the Emperor and he spoke highly about the valor of Kefelew and his men. Kefelew handed Tegegne Busera's machinegun and was pardoned by the Emperor. When Hailu came forward to express his loyalty through war songs, General Abebe told the Emperor about the valor and loyalty of Hailu. The Emperor recognized a member of the Imperial Bodyguard who was with him during the return journey from the Battle of Maichew.

"Who is your father?" the Emperor asked him.

Hailu enumerated his ancestors in a way that showed his familial relationship to the Emperor. The Emperor seemed to be impressed. He was forming a new government from the fragments of the pre-war government. He knew that he needed loyal army units and a well-established security force for himself. He was picking patriots without strong loyalties to the legendary patriotic generals while on his journey from Gojjam to Addis Ababa, to serve him as the nucleus for his national security apparatus. "You will join our convoy and come to Addis Ababa," ordered the Emperor.

Hailu felt honored.

Hailu left to Addis Ababa that same day with the Emperor's entourage. Meseret and Mahlet followed after a week.

Mahlet and Meseret asked Tekle to look for Giovanni. They found him preparing to go to Debre Birhan after he got amnesty.

Mahlet and Giovanni got married that week.

9

When Meseret and Mahlet reached Addis Ababa, Eleni, Meseret's mother was there to receive them. She was dressed like the Europeans and they only identified her when she came, clasped them and kissed them.

Eleni also saw for the first time her grandson, Meshageria Samuel. He was very small and retarded. Many children born during the war had been affected by the intensive chemical onslaught by fascist Italy. Rivers and soil were poisoned and remained toxic for a long time; many of the victims of the poisoning were children.

Life in Addis Ababa was full of new things for Meseret and Mahlet. It did not take them long to adapt to city life. During her stay in Addis Ababa, Meseret remembered the preaching of Kahn Yohannes about temptation. When they were in Debre Birhan, Hailu bought himself a khaki coat, trousers and a bonnet, which resembled the English uniform. He would also sip Italian wine once in a while. She had changed her traditional dress for factory products, while Mahlet adopted the European style of dress.

Meseret would not attend meetings and ceremonies commemorating the 5-year struggle against Italian fascism. Her interest was sharpened when Hailu brought her the news that Ethiopia declared war on Italy, Germany, and Japan in December 1942. Hailu read excerpts from a cable from the American President Roosevelt to the Emperor Haile Selassie on 16 December.

"By virtue of this historical declaration the first nation to be freed from the yoke of Axis oppression has joined its forces with those of the United Nations in this great struggle to preserve the freedom of mankind."

When Meseret passed from Arat Kilo to Sidist Kilo, she would try imagining what the replica of the Axum obelisk might have looked like before the Italians turned it to ashes. Tekle had shown her where it stood after she came to Addis Ababa. Sometimes she passed the Post Office building in Arada she would try to picture what the Monument for the Star of the Arch of the Covenant might have looked like before the Italians removed and hid it. Once Tekle showed her the shape of the star of the Arch of the Covenant that stood as a symbol mounted in front of Mercedes automobiles made in Germany.

Meseret truly believed that the ideas that were preached by Kahn Yohannes and the Sheik of the Mosque in Yifat were words of truth. They have given them the strength to survive the chemical warfare and fascist atrocities during a long drawn out war of resistance.

On April 12, 1945, USA President Roosevelt died and Ethiopians mourned him. He was their friend and their hope. The Ethiopian Radio repeatedly transmitted the speech of USA President Roosevelt made when the Fascist Party of Italy deposed Mussolini in July 1943 and arrested him.

"Mussolini came to the reluctant conclusion that the jig was up. He could see the shadow of the long arm of justice; but he and his fascist gangs will be brought to book and punished for their crimes against humanity. No criminal will be allowed to

escape by the expedient of resignation. So our terms to Italy are still the same as our terms to Germany and Japan; Unconditional surrender."

Meseret cried for long and lit a candle in his memory to St. Mary of Zion (Tsion Mariam). She remembered that after this speech by Roosevelt, Mussolini with the help of the Germans had been reinstated as Italy's leader. Now with the death of Roosevelt, she sensed how the enemies of humanity would be happy. She was enraged and she cried passionately.

In Italy, Mussolini, who had been a paid agent by the British during the First World War and later on a fascist leader was captured by the Italian Liberation Fighters fifteen days after the death of President Roosevelt. He was shot and hung upside down, befitting his cowardice. The Ethiopians celebrated the day. They felt not only them, but also Roosevelt had been avenged.

That day, during the celebration of the death of Mussolini, Generals Kassa and Seyoum, the veterans of the Ethiopian Christmas offensive in 1936 stood at the right side of the Emperor. Generals Abebe, Amoraw and many others who were the veterans of the patriotic battlefront stood at the left side of the Emperor. The rank and file of the patriotic armies paraded in front of them.

From afar, Meseret observed the patriots passing in a military parade. They were not commemorating the martyred millions, but eulogizing themselves encouraged unknowingly by their enemies. She saw Kefelew parading leading his army. He was wearing short trousers that showed his thin legs. The resemblance led Meseret to recall Gizachew

Haile, who was assassinated by Italian hirelings in the same week Samuel, her late husband and father of her child was killed. Then followed a parade led by Tessema, the commander of the Yifat army. He was not carrying his machinegun anymore; he now had a pistol on his hip, and was leading his soldiers with pride. Meseret remembered how he used to fire his machinegun from the hip. She smiled. Istefo, his brother was not around. Meseret remembered her uncle, Commander Beshah. She imagined how he would have been in this parade had he still been alive. She sobbed. She imagined what Samuel would have said if he had been there. Her tears started to flow down her cheeks. The representatives of the armies from all provinces were parading past. It seems endless. The soldiers who had served for five, four, three, two or one year in the patriotic armies were competing with each other for the Emperor's attention, along with those who came from exile. Meseret found this deeply disturbing.

The radio transmitted repeatedly the speech of USA President Roosevelt made when the Fascist Party of Italy deposed Mussolini in July 1943 and arrested him. Amharic translations of the speech were aired in between.

Tekle watched a former fascist spy who was stationed in Addis Ababa. He was looking with contempt and smiling. He came towards Tekle. He greeted him casually and said "Mussolini is dead and he deserved it and Petro Badoglio has replaced him as the Italian leader."

"Is that the same Badoglio who ordered chemical warfare on Ethiopia and responsible for the death of millions?" Tekle could not help but burst out.

"Yes."

Tekle had hoped that President Roosevelt's promise that all criminals would be brought to justice would be fulfilled. Now his belief had been shattered with the death of Roosevelt.

"The partisans who hanged Mussolini spared Graziani," continued the fascist agent, teasing Tekle.

Tekle felt that General Abebe and the patriotic forces were in danger. He felt bad intent amongst the fascists and the bandas against the patriotic army commanders and their soldiers.

Meseret went to her home to commemorate the day alone. Once at home the memory of Samuel and her uncle Beshah engulfed her. She sobbed for long time. She imagined the millions who died in the north and the southeast in Ogaden, Sidama and during the patriotic war affecting the whole of Ethiopia by the sustained chemical onslaught. She knew that the braves and the most astute were all dead... martyrs for their country, religion and way of life.

Meseret lit a candle for Mary of Zion in memory of the martyrs. She remembered the Ethiopian friends during the wartime black, white, yellow, and most of all Sylvia Pankhurst. She lit another candle for Mary of Zion in their memory.

She lit the third candle for the wellbeing of Mahlet and Giovanni and their descendants. She felt she has accomplished what she had to do. She rose up.

She was going out of the house when she met Tekle and greeted him. He was carrying a candle. "On victory day, we should remember the martyrs not eulogize the survivors," said Meseret.

Tekle showed his agreement by moving his head up and down. He felt that Ethiopia's hope of bringing to justice the perpetrators of chemical warfare and those who massacred millions of people were buried with Roosevelt. Meseret's hand was placed on the head of her son, Meshageria Samuel, standing beside her.

Tekle looked at Meseret and smiled. He saw that soon Meseret and Hailu would be blessed with a son or a daughter. He congratulated Meseret.

The end

www.ingramcontent.com/pod-product-compliance
Lightning Source LLC
Chambersburg PA
CBHW060503090426
42735CB00011B/2096